SURVIVE

Tales of Man versus Weather, Wilderness, and Wild Animals

Edited by
Lamar Underwood

FALCONGUIDES

GUILFORD, CONNECTICUT
HELENA, MONTANA

AN IMPRINT OF GLOBE PEQUOT PRESS

FALCONGUIDES®

Publication Data

s, weather, and wilderness / edited by Lamar Underwood.

ood, Lamar.

2013010057

d States of America

5 4 3 2 1

To those worldwide instructors of survival skills, basic and advanced, whose efforts save lives and make the great outdoors more enjoyable for all.

CONTENTS

Acknowledgments vii

Introduction ix

The Unridden Realm, Andy Martin 1

Siqinyasaq Tatqiq: Moon of the Returning Sun,
  Richard K. Nelson 27

Treat It Right, Scott McMillion 55

Land of Trembling Earth, Charles Elliott 81

All Gold Canyon, Jack London 107

Bending the Map, Laurence Gonzales 133

White Shark, Archibald Rutledge 159

A Plan to Recover the Trail, Cary J. Griffith 171

The Dandy Pat, Hugh Fosburgh 191

A Walk in the Park, Jill Fredston 201

Out of the Shadows, John Haines 229

Copyrights and Permissions 242

About the Editor 244

ACKNOWLEDGMENTS

This book exists because of the editorial skills and downright persistence of Imee Curiel. Her contributions from ideas to printed page have created a virtual editorial life support system that made this book happen. I would also like to thank Jessica Haberman for launching the project at Globe Pequot. A special thanks goes out to all our contributors, their publishers, and their agents and representatives for allowing us to present their stories.

INTRODUCTION

A recent news story reported that a father (an Air Force veteran) and his two sons had died on a simple hike in Missouri. With their yellow Labrador retriever, they were on a popular trail about 110 miles from St. Louis. Darkness and a January storm were approaching. They became disoriented, moving deeper into the woods instead of back to their starting point. They were not prepared to spend a night in the forest in the freezing rain. They died of exposure. The Lab survived and was found near the bodies. Even without flashlights, food and clothing, a good knife, and some matches might have produced a different ending to this tragic event.

We hate to see good people get hurt, and we really jump to attention when we learn these folks were pursuing outdoor activities we're keen on ourselves. Backcountry exploration, mountaineering, river running, swimming, surfing—outdoor adventures aren't necessarily dangerous. But, as aviators like to say, while not inherently dangerous they can be terribly unforgiving of carelessness, incapacity, or neglect. Whatever the cause—bad weather, poor planning, gross incompetence, or plain old bad luck—under the right (or perhaps wrong) circumstances, a routine hike can turn into a disaster.

Most of us who are addicted to outdoor recreation try to be prepared with gear and know-how. We're out to have fun, not prove we can live through the kinds of survival situations written about by famous pioneering explorers. Still, we can lose our way, be hit by deadly storms, make mistakes, and injure ourselves out where help is far away and out of touch. Perhaps in many cases that is why we're out there in the first place: to feel the edge of danger, to escape the humdrum of everyday life.

And surely that is why we turn to reading outdoor survival stories. We want to know what went wrong, how these ordinary people made it through—or didn't, as the case may be.

In the stories selected for this anthology, you may find yourself sharing the experiences of people who do your own outdoor thing—camping, hiking, gold-panning, surfing. You know what it's like out there, and I guarantee that these tales will strike a chord of recognition. You may also learn something about what it's like to experience survival as an everyday fact of life, where harsh conditions and looming predators make seeing the next day far from a foregone conclusion. You'll envision yourself at the scene, experience the "felt life" that comes from good reading. And you'll understand that no matter how tranquil the scene, disaster can strike in a heartbeat.

Danger waits on the icy, windswept tundra and its frozen shores; in lush southern swamplands and in swift rivers that cut through desert canyons; on the slopes of mountains thrusting from wild and uncut forests; in remote forests where scattered lakes dot the sweep of dense pine, birch, and alder. Out here, other than the cries of birds, the only sounds are made by the wind or water lapping at the shores of lakes, rushing through rapids, or sliding deep and dark against snags of fallen branches.

No matter the peace of heart found here, certain dangers lurk beside every trail, every campsite. Ignore them at your risk.

The challenges in these tales aren't from mysterious islands oceans away. The settings bear recognizable names. Sometimes the people in these dramas are living in the wilderness, where every day can be a battle for survival. But for many, danger catches up with them while they are pursuing favorite outdoor pursuits on familiar terrain—hiking in Glacier National Park, canoeing in Minnesota's Boundary Waters Area, skiing in Alaska's coastal ranges, fishing in Georgia's Okefenokee Swamp, surfing the great waves off Oahu's North Shore, to name a few. Like the ill-fated hikers in Missouri, these adventurous individuals ran into dangers they never expected and were ill prepared to meet.

Suddenly the unforgiving moment strikes. With survival at stake, they must fight for their lives.

I love the wild places and intend to keep enjoying them every chance I get. And if I'm careful—and perhaps a little bit lucky—I'll never have a survival story of my own to write for a book like this.

I'll stick to my reading.

LAMAR UNDERWOOD
JANUARY 2013

THE UNRIDDEN REALM
ANDY MARTIN

We've all seen the mountainous waves, looming over beaches around the world. We've seen them in the movies, that is, and on television and the Web and in magazine photographs. And we watch, in awe, as surfboarders ride these impossibly high and steep liquid mountains in maneuvers that take them to death-defying rendezvous with crashing tons of water. Surfers, whether they attain the superstar class of skills or just aspire to riding a couple of decent waves off usually benign stretches of beach, are a worldwide cult of adrenaline seekers. They scan the weather reports and updates on wave action with intensity, longing for the swells and breakers that will give them good rides. Among the breeding grounds for the biggest waves of all—the ones we see most in film and print—are Sunset and Waimea Bay Beaches on the North Shore of Oahu in the Hawaiian Islands.

In winter this area becomes a magnet for surfing's top stars, wannabes, and everyday folks who want to see the waves—and watch the seemingly suicidal boarders who venture onto them. In January 1985 Waimea became the site of a surfboarding duel between two of the greatest surfers in the world.

Ken Bradshaw and Mark Foo had been battling wave to wave in contests throughout the 1980s. Now they were to meet on some of the biggest waves ever recorded. The drama of that day—and the entire battle for recognition between the two men—is superbly told in Andy Martin's book Stealing the Wave. Here's what it's like to ride the waves where surfboarding becomes far more than a sport or a passion but a battle for survival.

■ ■ ■

Foo had flu. He was in bad shape. By 18 January 1985 he had been battling against flu for ten days and he couldn't shake it. He had only been in the water once in all that time. He was feeling rusty, below par, and altogether unfit. It was a bad day to wake up to what he later described as "a date with destiny."

• • •

Bradshaw, on the other hand, was optimal. He was always optimal. He showered in the outside cubicle with the slatted wooden door, singing "It takes a lot of skill and courage unknown, ha-ha-hum . . ." He was clean, he was healthy, he didn't have a germ on him. He slurped down his smoothie, with an extra dose of wheat germ and ginseng, put on his best shorts, took his best big-wave board, the tangerine-coloured one (that logo, BRADSHAW—HAWAII, still made him feel good every time), and strapped it down on top of his car, hopped in and drove off, whistling. He was cool, he was composed, he was anticipating great things. It had only taken one look out of the window that morning, as the sun came up, to tell him that this was going to be a special day. Sunset was already maxed out, a chaos of breaking waves and an immense meringue of white water. There was only one place that would be working today. One place that *he* would be working. It was his place, the Bay he had made his own.

• • •

Foo yawned and dragged himself out of bed. Stupid to be out partying the night before when he was already ill. But he felt it was all part of the job once he'd finished recording one of his radio shows. He opened the door on to the balcony and gazed out across Three Tables, just around the point from Waimea. Twelve-to-fifteen-foot waves breaking on the reef. He knew, like Bradshaw, that there could be only one place worth looking at today. Amazing, he thought to himself, that it takes so much energy to make it show. Places like Sunset, Pipe and Haleiwa can all be totally out of control with close-out second reef sets—and still Waimea is barely aroused. It was truly a sleeping giant. And, in his judgement, it was probably still half asleep. The swell was not quite large enough to make the Bay break, as it ought to, in its classic big-wave form. So, in the light of all these considerations, Foo felt justified in taking a pill and sipping a glass of honey and lemon and slumping back on his bed for a while longer. After all, it had been a late night last night.

■   ■   ■

Bradshaw smiled as he got out of the car and took his board off the rack. He congratulated himself on getting to bed early the night before. He liked to describe himself as a "space cadet," disciplined, with good habits, and therefore ready and able to meet any challenge. He had become a vegetarian— a "lacto-ovo-vegetarian," to be precise (and he was never less than precise)—suspecting that too much meat slowed you down and made you too bulky. He looked down at his sculpted chest. Lots of hair, but not an ounce of fat on it, lean and mean, fat-free. It was not vanity, it was just pragmatism; you had to be in perfect condition to stand a chance of grappling with the biggest waves on the planet and coming out on top. He just prayed it would hit twenty today, the magic marker beyond which Waimea turns into the majestic and ravenous beast known as Real Waimea.

■   ■   ■

Foo snoozed. When he next looked out of the window it was around midday. He had to admit, the swell had been building, the sets were heavier, and he was pretty sure that the surf would meet the 18–20-foot minimum requirement. He wolfed a bun, a banana and two cups of coffee before grabbing in his 9-foot Lundy and crossing the street and walking the last few hundred yards down to the Bay. He could hear the noise of thunder. Every now and then the earth seemed to tremble beneath his feet as another wave hit the beach and exploded. He could still back out without losing face, he told himself. It would all depend on the conditions. They had to be right, because he wasn't. But as soon as he saw Waimea, as he came around the point, his mind was made up. As he wrote later in his article "Occurrence at Waimea Bay," "I was far from being in the most prepared state, but Waimea was doing it and there was only one guy in the line-up. I was out there."

The one guy in the line-up was, of course, Ken Bradshaw. Foo knew it had to be Bradshaw; he was the only one with the balls to be out there when it was like this. It was not classic Waimea, with waves like pyramids chugging in out of the Pacific and gradually walling up and folding. No, today Waimea was *untraditional*. Extreme west swell. The recent storm had dumped a lot of sand in the middle of the bay, making the place shallower, like a sand bar beachbreak, but much much bigger, so that the waves sucked up suddenly and pitched around precariously and toppled over. And the rip channeling out all the surplus water was working overtime as if a sorceror's apprentice had switched on an assembly line and cranked it up to maximum. It was made for Bradshaw, with that broad-shouldered muscular physique of his. But Foo knew he had to go out there and mix it with him. He kept on going, going down the concrete steps that led on to the beach. He could see the swell was still building: it was already beyond twenty, with some 25-foot sets at roughly twenty-minute intervals. Timing would be crucial.

While Foo was still thinking about things, checking timing and going through his loosening-up routine on the beach, Bradshaw had already been out for around three hours. He just couldn't help but think of the words of that good old song, "it takes a lot of skill and courage unknown to catch the last wave and ride it in ALONE. . . ." And that's just what he was: *alone*. Last man out. There had been a small crowd to start with, but everyone else had been gradually burned out. No one else could hack it out here. It was just too huge and unpredictable. People were being cleaned up and washed right in. Everyone, that is, except for one man. If anyone had caught the wave of the day, it had to be Bradshaw. He was on to everything that was half makeable, and he was making it. And now, since there was no one else left, everything was his for the taking. God, he loved Waimea. He thought of it as a giant toilet flushing away all the shit in life. Cleansing, purifying.

Sometimes he thought to himself, when he was out here, that no one else really existed. All those strange people you saw walking around town, doing things, well, they were just phantasms, illusions, they weren't real human beings at all; maybe they were androids, designed to test him in some way, to see if they could weaken him, distract him from his mission, cause him to swerve when he should be going in a straight line. It was the kind of insight you had in massive surf. Bradshaw felt a sense of enlightenment sweep over him, flooding him with knowledge and power. He checked his positioning, lining himself up with the church tower and the tree on the cliff. What was the word? *Omniscience*. That was it. He savoured the idea. Sometimes—for a moment or two—he had the sensation that he had finally attained it. He could do no wrong. He had the feeling he was invulnerable and he was immortal. It was a good feeling. Today it struck him so clearly, so forcefully, that he knew it had to be right.

While he was being rolled around underwater—who knew which way was up any more?—Bradshaw was put in mind for a moment of that scene in *2001: A Space Odyssey*, in which an astronaut, venturing outside the vehicle, has his lifeline severed (by Hal the deranged computer) and tumbles chaotically through space until gradually he runs out of oxygen, his movements finally cease and he is encompassed by the infinite cold and darkness of the universe. His limbs jerking wildly as if controlled by an insane puppet master, Bradshaw struggled to comprehend what had gone wrong. His positioning had been perfect, nobody could fault him on positioning. He was right in the driving seat for anything in the 20–25-foot range. There was only one conclusion: he had been caught out, or rather caught inside, by a 30-footer, and spanked like an errant schoolchild. That was *interesting*. So the swell was still building. He continued spinning for a good long while, thinking to himself, hey, this is a heavy hold-down, must have been a serious 30-footer all right. This kind of rough treatment doesn't come around too often. Ah well, might as well enjoy it. It was sent to test me. *Go on, hit me again!*

When he finally popped up into the world above, Bradshaw had no idea where his board was. Then he saw it, or rather a part of it, and there was another part over there, and another. His best big-wave board had been shattered into orange shards. *Far out!*—that had been a tough old board, a three-stringer, built for endurance and resistance above all, and now it looked as if it had been fed through a wood-chipper. Well, there was nothing for it now but to swim in. He could no long "ride the last wave" but he could swim through it, bodysurf maybe. Bradshaw wasn't about to make the kind of elementary error Woody Brown and Dickie Cross had made in the 1940s and try to come in through the channel. That was out of the question. The rip was just enormous. Anyway he liked to come in through the breaking waves; that was the only way to have any fun when you'd lost your board. A bit of ducking and diving. You'd see turtles and dolphins doing it all the time at Waimea so he saw no reason why a human being couldn't do it as well.

He knew there was only one way in—the narrow exit lane along the rocks at the east end of the Bay, wedged between the point and the beach. All Bradshaw had to do was keep powering through the shorebreak. He charged it, head down, full throttle, maximum power. To his surprise the surging rip current kept on tugging him around, away from the beach, towards Coffin Corner, the great shipwrecking rocks to the west at the far end of the Bay. He kept on churning his massive steam-shovel arms, kicking those thick tree-trunk legs, but it was no good, he was going sideways and backwards. That damn rip had more of a pull than he'd encountered before. There was no point trying to fight it now. Eddie had said: "If you can't make it through before the river [some 100 yards from the rocks], you're not going to make it through." He'd just have to go round and try again.

So Bradshaw angled out with the channel—that was easy, you could hardly help swimming that way!—and then geared himself up again for the swim in. He took a couple of medium-sized waves on the head, floundering a little, then came up and, blowing hard, drove for the way out. Again, incredibly, he felt himself sliding away in the wrong direction, as if being towed off by an invisible hand. Again Coffin Corner beckoned. With a perfectly justifiable sense of *déjà vu*, he steered for the channel once more, paddling out into the immense and inexhaustible Pacific again.

It was about now that Bradshaw started to feel a faint sense of fatigue. It didn't happen to him too often. He realised that he had been surfing for several hours even before swimming a couple of times around the Bay. It came to him then, and the idea was shocking, that he actually had limits, and that he was starting to run up against them. *Fascinating*, he said to himself, like an alien observing some eccentric human trait—this sense that he was running out of gas, running on empty, never had *that* before! His whole life was built on the twin pillars of absolute strength and unquenchable stamina. The idea of defeat entered his mind for the first time and he fought to hold it back. Was this what fear was like? Well, there was nothing for it now but to go through the whole procedure again. His third lap of the Bay. He had no better idea. There was only one way to go so he had better go for it.

A couple more big ones drilled him down and drove him forwards. He came up in the middle of a lull. For once the great heaving, howling, bay-sized Suds-o-matic that was Waimea paused in mid-cycle, gathering its strength for another onslaught. Bradshaw put his big bull head down and windmilled his arms around one more time and tried to hug the rocks. Again he felt the gut-wrenching drag of the rip sweeping back into the middle of the Bay. He was low on energy but he dug for shore, grinding out the strokes, like a man pulling himself up a rope, hand over hand, up and away from the yawning abyss under his feet, but all the while aware that the rope was fraying and unravelling under the pressure.

People on the beach had begun to assume Bradshaw was a goner. It was like seeing Houdini go under for longer than five minutes. Banzai Betty, who rented me the room at Backyards, stood watching him and thought, "No one has ever swum more than twice around the Bay in conditions like these and survived. It is just physically impossible." She felt a twinge of sympathy for Bradshaw, even though, when she had once courageously paddled out at Waimea on a big day, he had seen her coming and raised a sarcastic eyebrow: "You're coming out? I'm going in—it must be too small!"

When he dragged himself up on the sand, a lifeguard came running up to him. To shake him by the hand? Bradshaw pushed him away. He didn't need oxygen, he was alive, wasn't he? He strode up the beach, for once rather enjoying the feel of solid stuff beneath his feet, amid applauding spectators. It was probably one of the most epic feats of endurance ever witnessed at Waimea Bay, a saga of the will to survive. Bradshaw gritted his teeth, sucking in air through his nose, and stuck out his chin, as if to say, *Look, no problem, business as usual, that wasn't so bad*. At the same time the look he gave everyone defied anyone else to go out there and give it a whirl. Then he saw the Kid doing his stretching routine on the dune.

There was something about that warm-up routine that never failed to rile him, this big public display, as if Foo were saying, *Hey, look at me everybody, here I am, Mark Foo—the great Foo!—I'm getting warmed up now, I'm getting ready to go out*. Surely nobody was going to go out now. He, Bradshaw, had proved that it was too big to handle. If he couldn't make it, nobody could. End of story.

Foo looked up again to see if Bradshaw was OK. He knew that he was going to make it. He hadn't even begun to worry about him drowning out there. As a combination of experience, water knowledge and sheer guts, it was an impressive display, he had to admit. He would have put money on Bradshaw making it through, though. He always did, that was the way he was. He was solid, dependable, rugged. He just lacked imagination, that was all. He was like an old warhorse that bullets and cannonballs seemed to bounce off. That was Bradshaw's Law—survival. Foo always felt that even if he came up quietly behind him one day and walloped him over the head with something good and heavy it would do no more than rile him.

But Foo's instinct told him that you had to do something more than just survive out there. You had to do it with style, with finesse, with a degree of savvy and sophistication that was surely beyond the wit of the old warrior. So what if Bradshaw hadn't been able to make much of those waves? Foo glanced at the ocean again. He was confident he could get inside some of these big fat juicy smokers and get the hell out again unscathed. And now Bradshaw, that great obdurate, stubborn obstacle, was safely out of the way, there was nothing and nobody to stop him. This was his big chance to make it count and rebrand himself as a big-wave maestro. No more "small-wave specialist" jibes. No more "Kid."

"Where there is an opening at Waimea," he would subsequently write, "you have to make your move." This was his opening. It was destiny calling. He didn't particularly *want* to go, he just knew he *had* to go. He was far beyond any idea of choosing.

Foo knelt down, picked up his board and went down the hill to the edge of the water. James Jones and the bodyboarder J. P. Patterson were already paddling out just ahead of him. He flung himself into the steaming broth of the shorebreak and paddled forcefully into the channel and Ace Cool followed right behind him, trying to stay in his slipstream. Ace had been watching Foo: if Foo was going out, he was going out. The funny thing was that Foo had never really checked the surf at close quarters. He was concentrating on his own moves. He didn't like to watch the waves too much in case it stopped him going out. So when Foo was followed out by Ace it was the blind leading the blind. Now there were four men out. Bradshaw shook his head up on the dune and looked grim. They were all dead meat. If he couldn't make it, nobody could. Of that he was certain. It was curtains for Foo.

Bradshaw never admitted to fear. It was a point of principle with him. He always said if he was afraid he'd never go out (but since he was afraid of nothing he always would go). Foo, on the other hand, regularly acknowledged fear. Especially at the Bay. Now, as he paddled out, he was starting to regret not having checked out the surf properly. He could taste the faint, bitter tang of imminent peril on his tongue and he could feel the fluttering of the great void that loomed up inside him as a reminder of the immense nothingness that awaited him somewhere down the line. Maybe not too far down. Foo took his regular slow wide-angled course around the back of the break, through the middle of the Bay, so as to prepare himself for what lay ahead.

Now he would have to look at the surf, from very close quarters. Sometimes too close. "We all quickly realised that this was no ordinary big day." All the waves were ledging up, hitting a fully vertical angle, as perpendicular as lighthouses, far too soon. There seemed to be no chance of getting into any of them, no ramp, no entry lane. The four men remained wide, out in the channel, not even on the shoulder, apprehensive of the sheer refractory trickiness of these waves, with a geometry none of them had seen before at Waimea. Not one of them seemed in the least rideable. And even then they had to keep swinging out and around crazy, lumbering, lopsided waves, the kind of waves that defined "gnarly," that were jacking up and pitching over in an area that would normally be considered "the safety zone." What they all quickly realised was that, on this day, there was no such thing as a safety zone at Waimea. The field of play had had all its lines washed out, erased. Twenty-five-footers were springing up almost at random and taking over the entire Bay, leaving no breathing space. It was the kind of day that Woody Brown and Dickie Cross had once encountered and found beyond their powers.

The interval between the biggest sets was going down all the time. In other words, the number of extremely large and terrifying breakers was going up. There was one solid 30-foot wave that had all four men scratching to get up the face and over the top before it went into meltdown. As it lurched by under him Foo had the opportunity to see it break, seemingly in slow motion: "It was a moment I will never forget. The monster pitched up and out and turned into the biggest tube you could ever imagine. On other days at Waimea, Sunset, Pipeline or Honolua, I've seen some big holes . . . but nothing like this. It looked like a huge cavern with half the ocean as its roof and sides." This trembling, thundering sine curve seemed to Foo so overwhelmingly powerful that he had the impression that the water was no longer a liquid element at all but rather something solid and hard, "like concrete." *The hard and the strong cannot stand against it.* The wave was cemented into his imagination like architecture. It was far far in excess of anything that could reasonably be attempted and brought off.

All four men looked back respectfully, and with an enormous sense of relief, at the wave as it rolled on by. James Jones turned to Foo and said that he had taken off on a wave like that on the morning of the 1974 Smirnoff contest (also held at Waimea), got tumbled and held down and had almost died, and that he would never try one like it again. Foo nodded in agreement. Jones was right. He realised then that "there was no way to ride such a wave, no matter how long a board, no matter how early you got in, there was just too much energy and moving water." Perhaps by way of easing the tension, Jones hollered out to Ace, "Hey, Alec, if you had caught that one you would have had the record."

Ace Cool, everyone knew—he had made *sure* that everyone knew—was fixated on capturing the biggest wave. That was his one aim in life—claiming the undisputed big one. Sheer size mattered to Ace, as it mattered to all of them—it was just that he was more outspoken about it. And yet, when it had come along, he too had been glad to get the hell out of the way of it. The desire to score the mightiest wave ever ridden by man constantly battled against the flickering desire for self-preservation. Yes, he would have had the record if he'd ridden it, but there was no way he was even going to touch a brutal bucking rabid maniac of a sidewinding wave like that one. It all came down to selection.

It was shortly after that colossus passed them by that Foo heard screaming on the beach and the massed honking of car horns. He looked towards the crowd that had gathered there—it seemed a long way off, almost like another dimension, although only half a mile or so distant—and they were pointing out over his shoulder. There was a 25–30-foot wave behind him and Foo scrambled to get over the top of it. Is that all? he said to himself. Piece of cake. What were they getting so worked up about? And then he looked up at the horizon. Way up at where the horizon used to be.

What Mark Dambrowski saw a couple of miles away made him reach for the phone in the lifeguard tower. Aged thirty-one, he had trained under Eddie Aikau and thought he had seen it all at Waimea—until approximately 3 p.m. on the afternoon of 18 January 1985. "Get the chopper in the air," he screamed down the phone, "there's four guys in the water and not one of them is going to get out of there alive. You're going to be picking up bodies." In those days there was a rescue helicopter based at the fire house opposite Foodland, less than a mile to the east of the Bay.

Foo called it "the beast" or "the thing." It made all the other waves that had passed them by that day look feeble by comparison. The effect it had on Foo was this: it made him laugh out loud. It was a freak, the mother of all freaks: an impossible wave, unbelievable, insane, a caricature of a wave drawn by a lunatic, straining up into the sky. A King Kong among waves. Technically this was a "rogue" wave, resulting from the union of two or more waves; but this one was not so much a rogue as Public Enemy No. 1. Call it what you will—it was coming straight at them. Estimates of its size vary. Foo called it more than twice the size of anything else they had seen that day, which would make it around 60–70 feet from base to toppling crest. Others called it eighty. All agreed that they had never seen anything like it on the North Shore. Perhaps it was comparable to the wave that Woody Brown and Dickie Cross had seen and had claimed to be 100 feet. It was still a good couple of hundred yards away and already it was standing up and feathering at the top. It was impossible to see anything else. There was nothing but this immense wave. To Foo the sky had become liquid, the sheer presence of water filled his whole perceptual field. He began to feel that he did not exist any more, he was nothing, nothing existed, nothing except this all-encompassing immensity.

James Jones was already steaming for the horizon, with a view to making it over the top. He saw it first. Foo was in the worst possible position: he was the furthest over, on the inside, more exposed than anyone to the severest forces. He knew as soon as he saw "the thing" that there was no chance whatever of getting to it before it broke, so he turned towards the centre of the Bay and paddled for the channel, reckoning that the aftermath would be at its least potent in this area. What he didn't know was that this megawave was about to break from top to bottom across the entire width of the Bay. It was the biggest close-out at Waimea that anyone had ever seen.

Standing up on the dune, shading his eyes from the sun, Bradshaw gazed out to sea with mixed feelings of admiration, reverence, sorrow and satisfaction. The ocean was playing fair, without fear or favour. Everyone who had foolishly, vainly, ventured out there, despite the warning that his own experience had offered, was about to be erased from contention. He turned to the white-haired, one-eyed Peter Cole, sitting on the bonnet of his car and timing the set intervals, and said, "That is undisputedly the largest wave anybody has ever had to deal with." Cole, at fifty-four a tall, loping, James Stewart figure, one of the grand old men of Waimea, who had delivered a eulogy at Eddie Aikau's funeral, thought he had seen everything—the massive swells of 1969, the Smirnoff in 1974—now he had to revise his "everything" significantly upwards. Even he, temperamentally conservative in his esti-mations, had to admit that 18 January 1985 was an exceptional kind of a day. His single functioning eye followed the surfers like a telescope and registered the not very surprising fact that they had all just disappeared, steamrollered by the great wave.

"The beast" had metamorphosed from a lumbering, tow-ering cliff-face into "a thundering avalanche of white water" (in Foo's words). You couldn't surf it: there was no way over or around it. The only way through was under. Wherever they were going, all four souls bailed, sucked in their last mouthfuls of air and dived immediately for the bottom, fugi-tives from the thrust of the primal wave. Wedged on the sea-bed, Foo looked up and watched in wonder as an extremely large inverted tornado ghosted by above him. The thing he feared was what would come behind it: a second successive hold-down, on this scale, would surely finish them. All four men had been wearing leashes, attaching their boards to their ankles, like a prison ball and chain. But when, almost miracu-lously, they floated up to the surface, still breathing, only the leashes remained—all the boards, bar one, had been swept away. The exception was Foo's. His leash had held. That had been one all-time mother of a rogue wave—but only one. He slid gratefully back on to his gun.

"What kind of leash you got on," said J. P. Patterson, resentfully, "a chain?" The other three, Jones, Patterson,

Cool, had no cards left to play; they struck out for shore, leaving Foo all alone in the middle of the Bay.

Foo was the last man out, just as Bradshaw had been earlier in the day. Then it had been Foo who was watching from the shore; now it was Bradshaw. Their positions had been precisely reversed. It was the Kid who was living out Bradshaw's fantasy for him—to catch the last wave and ride it in alone. Bradshaw could no longer delude himself into thinking that he was the last man left alive in a world which had been flooded by the great oneness. He had to concede that now there were two men at least, two who moved upon the face of the deep.

The helicopter had taken less than five minutes, after Dambrowski's call, to get in the air and race over to the Bay. They knew that the wave had eaten everyone up, so they were relieved to see all four men below, still alive. James Jones, with fifteen years of big-wave experience behind him, didn't hesitate: as soon as they lowered the basket he hopped right in, grateful for the ride. Ace, too proud to take the easy way out, opted to swim in, but got trapped in the shorebreak and was being tugged around towards the rocks. The helicopter lowered the basket to him again. *D'you want it this time?* Ace wanted it all right, and was reaching up to pull himself in when another of the outrageous close-out sets barrelled on through and smacked right into him. The crew kept on lowering the basket and every time Ace tried to climb in another wave dragged him off again, sucking him towards Coffin Corner. Finally he did the only thing he could do: he clung on to the basket by his fingertips, yelling, "Go on, get me out of here!" As they were reeling him in another wave, as if reluctant to let him go, smashed into him and rocked the basket and shook up the whole helicopter. But this time the leash held and Ace was airlifted out, dangling and spinning on the end of the basket. The helicopter dropped him off and came back for Patterson, who had retrieved his board but had nowhere left to go.

That left only Foo. The last man out. The crew called out to him to grab the basket, his ticket back to safety and sanity. But Foo ignored them. He was scared, but he was still alive. He was still on his board. The Kid waved them away imperiously. He was surfing all alone in closed-out Waimea and, having seen what he was up against, was fully aware of the seriousness of his position. But how often did opportunities like this come along? So this was what destiny felt like. He'd often wondered. Being part of "the Plan," some higher cosmic irony. Big Waimea and no one else out, not even Bradshaw. Bradshaw, he knew, was marooned on the beach, bereft of an operational board. Foo had to admit that this was an additional incentive. Any wave he caught now would be like a dagger into the heart of Bradshaw. He would naturally feel that it was his wave, part of his personal collection, one of his harem, and that Foo had stolen it from under his nose. It was the thought of Bradshaw pacing up and down on the beach, grinding his teeth in frustration, that suddenly made Foo feel like a thief, casing the joint. He was stealing waves and it felt good. His only anxiety, at this point, was that the security measures at Waimea were severe and potentially lethal. There were good reasons to keep your hands off and behave. And, meanwhile, that helicopter basket being dangled in front of his face looked mighty tempting.

Foo had an idea that it would be advisable, in the circumstances, to get back to the beach. But he knew he had to do it on the back of a wave, not cradled in a basket. That was his vocation, his duty, his fate; he couldn't shirk it. Anyhow, he had a point to make, no matter that there might be a high price to pay for making it. For years he had been aiming for just this moment, never quite knowing if it would ever come, and now it had come and he was ready. The flu didn't seem to be bothering him any more. He had come out from under "the beast" in one piece, in good shape, and this was his big chance. Foo had worked out a reasonable cat-and-mouse-style plan (in which he was the mouse). He was going to keep a sharp weather eye out for the big close-out sets and paddle out over them (if he could) and then scoot back to the line-up in the hope of picking up a wave of more manageable proportions.

It was a good plan and it might have worked on any other day but this. More homicidal waves kept him sprinting for the horizon, but the intervals between major sets were now so short that Foo had no time to get back to the line-up before another big one forced him way outside all over again. The sets just kept on coming. There was no stopping them. The helicopter came back for Foo. He had no choice. There was no way he was ever going to get in; even he had to realise that now and throw in the towel. It was no loss of face. Everyone would agree he had been a plucky little devil, but this was the end of the road. They lowered the basket and shoved it in his face. Foo flat out ignored them. He stuck to his damn plan, even though he knew it was stupid and there was not a chance of it ever working out. He ought to take the ride, he knew. It was the only sensible course of action. But he couldn't back down now. The rational self-preserving side of his being cried out to him to hop into the basket.

That basket was as tempting as a bouquet of flowers to a bee. But Foo willed himself to shut it out of his mind. The irrational wave-accumulating side of his personality asserted itself: *Forget the chopper! Damn the basket! Find a wave to hitch a ride on!* The helicopter continued to hover overhead, as if to remind him of everything he was missing.

If he couldn't get an inside wave, he would have to go outside. Foo was somewhere in the middle of the Bay when a set approached. He drove for the first wave in the set, a certain left. But it started sucking out and going over before he could get on to it, so he pulled back. But he knew there was another one behind it. He calculated that even if it was bigger than the first wave in the set, it had to be breaking in deeper water after the first wave had broken and that might just give him a shot. Part of his theory was correct. The wave was big all right, but it held up and didn't fold over too soon. He had a window. He steered into position for take-off. The wave lifted him up towards heaven. Then he saw the whole thing hollowing out under him—as the last one had done—and going concave, bending right over like the sting of a very large scorpion. But now he had no choice—he had to keep on stroking, driving forwards. He had gone past the point of no return, too late to back out now. So he did the only thing he could do, which was to push up with his arms and spring to his feet.

He knew what was coming: a freefall drop. When a wave is this concave there is no chance of the board sticking to the wave or the surfer sticking to the board; one of them has to give, or both simultaneously. Foo launched himself over the ledge and took off. He was in flight, riding his board as if it were a wing. But he wasn't exactly glued to it in the first place. And now he was coming unstuck. He and the board flew through the air, aiming at reconnecting with the face further down, at a more rideable angle. They both flew well, Foo and the board, over the best part of 25 feet in a downward direction, but they parted company somewhere down the line. "Technically and mentally," Foo wrote, "I kept it all together," and maybe so, but unless he could actually walk on water, Foo was sunk, since he no longer had anything solid under his feet to ride on.

Somehow he managed to hook up with the board again, but he couldn't hold it. He crash-landed. That strange vision of Foo's—of the wave turning solid—seemed to have come true. Anyone who has gone off a high diving board knows: the faster you hit water, the harder it becomes. So it was that instead of penetrating the surface, Foo just bounced along it, skimming and skipping like a stone spinning across a lake. If only he could keep going like this all the way to shore, it would have been the next best thing. Then the wave folded over and "a good portion of the Pacific started to collapse on me." Foo felt the lip explode and he was right in the middle of it. He heard the sound of snapping—it was not his own body but the sound of his cherished 9-foot three-stringer Lundy giving up the ghost. Then, as if in slow motion, he saw the watch on his wrist being hoovered off and sucked into the maw. Finally he felt himself getting slurped up and spat out and hurled down—and this time he stayed down, a long way down.

For a while—a time hard to calculate, probably only half a minute or so, but played again and again endlessly in his memory—"Things turned grey." When he resurfaced, the helicopter was still there waiting. He board was gone. The chopper had won. The basket beckoned.

When Foo came to write the history of that day, he recalled each particular episode and element—"that gigantic tube," "that monster close-out," "that take-off," and so on. But what he emphasised more than anything else was a shift in his perspective. He used words on the page—for the first time, so far as I know—like "destiny," "fate," "the Plan." It is a strange sense that afflicts nearly everyone on the North Shore at one time or another: that of being caught up in something infinitely larger than themselves and yet not being an entirely meaningless chunk of debris, but rather an integral, functional entity within this great system. Suddenly it seemed to Foo as if contingency, the random realm of chance, had come to an end, and history, the orderly domain of the inevitable, had begun. Everything had a purpose. Raw, chaotic nature had been transformed into a meaningful, providential narrative. The way things happened was the way they were meant to be, the way they had to be. Foo had to be there, henceforth big waves were his domain, the Bay was his backyard. Telling the story was another part of "the Plan," too.

In "Occurrence at Waimea Bay"—syndicated in surf magazines around the world, from the US to Australia and Japan—Foo also coined a new phrase that gained a certain currency: "the unridden realm." That was Foo's name for the kind of wave he had taken off on, 35 foot and beyond. It was not meant to be. Certain waves cannot be ridden and that's that. To the question, "Who has ridden the biggest wave?" Foo answered, rather modestly: "Nobody." When he read Foo's story, this is the one part that Bradshaw definitely agreed with, especially the word *UNridden*. Some people were calling it "the biggest wave ever ridden." Well, that was just hype, the usual kind of propaganda and mystification you found in the magazines. As soon as Bradshaw tracked down the editor who had quoted Sir Edmund Hillary at the top of Foo's article—"Challenge is what makes men"—and added a totally spurious comparison between Foo and the mountaineer ("For Mark Foo, that sentiment manifested itself in this heroic ride"), he was going to straighten the guy out, harshly. It was time for some *rectification*.

The plain fact was, Bradshaw grumbled, "he never even *rode* the damn thing." He just took off on it. There's a world of difference. He was just showboating. It was the biggest wave *never* ridden. And he had to be picked up by helicopter. There was no way the Kid was going to swim three times around the Bay, he was too much of a ballerina for that, he expected to be chauffeured back home. Bradshaw read the "epilogue" again: "Since the events of this extraordinary afternoon, an unprecedented amount of media and public interest has been generated." *Damn right*, he thought, and *mainly by you*. Foo had engineered the whole story, and sponged up all the glory, and now he had the bare-faced audacity to speak of "destiny." It was yet another travesty.

There is a photograph of Bradshaw greeting Foo, shaking his hand as he returns triumphantly to the beach, "in a poignant moment of camaraderie." But the caption also suggests there is something other than pure camaraderie: a note of ambivalence: "Bradshaw congratulates Mark Foo not so much on his performance as for the fact that he made it in alive following the most intense session ever witnessed."

But whatever Bradshaw thought about it, from this day on Foo would always be categorised as, above all, a big-wave rider. A hellman, a fire-eater, one of the elite. Pretty soon he would be pronouncing in *Surfer* on the subject of "late take-offs" in heavy big-wave situations ("So much of surfing is mental, and heavy take-offs are more so than any other manoeuvre"). He name and reputation, his "destiny," were assured.

For the first time, Foo now started to talk in public about the realistic prospect of dying. He mentioned it one night at Sunset Beach Elementary School when he gave a speech to the kids. I couldn't help mentioning it to him myself from time to time in the years that followed the "Occurrence" article, the strong possibility that he might eventually run out of luck. He tended to reply: "If you want the ultimate thrill, you've got to be willing to pay the ultimate price." That was the rational capitalist in him speaking: he saw it as a fair exchange, a wave for a life. But he also thought that it would be better to die doing what he loved doing anyway. Another Foo-ism: "To go out surfing a monster wave—that would be a glamorous way to die." That was the applause-milking exhibitionist in him: he imagined dying, swan-like, on the biggest possible wave, spectacularly, with a final bow and a kiss to the audience. But behind all the bravado and the calculation, there was a deep and persistent sense of fatalism.

"You know I could die out there," he said to Sharlyn, shortly after 18 January.

"Then, don't do it," she said.

"Yeah, but I have to die sometime anyway," he replied.

In truth Foo was fond of the idea of going out with a bang rather than a whimper. "When the *Challenger* blew up," he said to me one day at the Bay, "everybody said it was a tragedy. But I thought: this was the moment they lived for. They died happy. That is the way I want to go. You can die at Waimea as easy as Outer Space."

Peter Cole, sitting on the bonnet of his car, looking at his watch, timing the sets and electing not to go out, said that what they had witnessed that afternoon was, more than anything else, "a lack of judgement." Bradshaw would have agreed. Perhaps even Foo would have conceded the point, but he would also have said that, if it was a mistake, it was nevertheless a mistake that had to be made. It was in the order of things to make precisely this mistake and no other. That was the way the cosmos was shaping that afternoon, so there was nothing to be gained in struggling against it and debating the point.

Cole also made two contradictory assertions. Firstly: "Big-wave surfing is one of the only applications of sport where records aren't broken as time goes on." The biggest waves he and Pat Curren had ever ridden, twenty years earlier—they were no different from these waves; it was scientifically impossible to surf anything bigger. And, secondly, in conclusion: "But who can say? The biggest wave ever hasn't been ridden yet." Both Foo and Bradshaw thought the same way. So did Ace Cool.

That night, the night of 18 January, Foo ended up at Ace Cool's house on the other side of Waimea. They watched a sketchy video recording of the afternoon's event and they agreed that neither of them had yet surfed the biggest wave. Nor had Bradshaw. It was still out there somewhere, still up for grabs. Everyone was still in the race. And yet there was a new degree of respect from Ace towards Foo. Maybe he had just been lucky, the way his leash had held, maybe it was fate;

either way, Ace needed some of it. One thing he noticed that Foo had been using—and he wondered if it could have given him a slight edge—was webbed gloves. They were supposed to help with paddling faster and, therefore, potentially, pulling off the bigger, faster waves.

The next day Ace went out and bought himself some webbed gloves.

EDITOR'S POSTSCRIPT

On December 23, 1994, surfing with Ken Bradshaw at a new hot spot called "Maverick's" at Half Moon Bay near San Francisco, Mark Foo was swept down by a tricky wave, huge but far smaller than many he had ridden before. He was seen to surface, then to disappear, for good. It was later discovered that the line that secured his board to his ankle, in a system he had developed, had become entangled in rocks. Unable to free himself, he met his death. He was thirty-six years old.

SIQINYASAQ TATQIQ:
MOON OF THE RETURNING SUN
RICHARD K. NELSON

It is my privilege to tell you with great enthusiasm and confidence that I have never read better prose about life in the Great Outdoors than the works of Richard Nelson. This selection is from his book Shadow of the Hunter: Stories of Eskimo Life, *a collection of Nelson stories based on actual experiences. Nelson lived with the Eskimo people of Alaska for fourteen months, sharing their experiences and knowledge, learning their way of life. Each story takes the reader into different times and realms of the Eskimo village of Tareogmiut, "people of the sea." While the stories are fictional, each represents ". . . a collage based on what is real." In the ancient and harsh environment these native people call home, the fight for survival is not a unique and sudden experience. It involves everyday life. All Nelson books are alive with great prose and the bite of authenticity. They include* Hunters of the Northern Ice, Hunters of the Northern Sea, *and his classic magnum opus,* The Island Within, *about living on an island in the Pacific Northwest. If you make* Shadow of the Hunter *and* The Island Within *your next two book purchases, I am confident you will thank me for sending you to them.*

. . .

It was near dawn, a few days past the New Year. A half-moon, low above the northern horizon, threw gray light across a featureless expanse of snow and ice. Featureless except for the silent cluster of houses set atop a low cliff where the tundra ended and long drifts sloped away to the ice-covered

Arctic Ocean. The houses made up a small Eskimo settlement called Ulurunik, "where-the-bank-crumbles." Thin streamers of smoke, glowing pale in the moonlight, trailed from each house and diffused into a haze above the ocean ice.

A large husky sat near the edge of the bank, its outline dimly silhouetted against the horizon. Then it stretched forward, lifted its head in a gentle arc, and began a deep, moaning howl. Its voice started low and hollow, rose slightly in pitch, then dropped and faded. The dog howled again, this time higher and louder, its head thrown back and wavering slowly from side to side. The third time it howled several dogs nearby rose to their feet and added their voices. This aroused still others, and the chorus spread, like a drift before a growing wind, until almost every dog in the village was howling. Their sound, eerie yet wild and beautiful, carried for miles through the clear, frigid air. After several minutes it faded away except for the shrill barks and howls of a few diehard pups. Silence closed back over the land.

A midwinter day was about to begin. Toward the southeast, pale blue was gradually spreading along the horizon, where flat tundra plain met arching sky. The sun would never appear above the horizon on this day, nor on many more that would follow. For more than two months each year it remained hidden from sight, unable to climb above the curved edge of the earth. Even during this season, however, the twilight was strong enough to create a "day" several hours long. What little light there was, the Eskimos appreciated to its fullest.

The dog that began the howling was one of eleven tethered alongside a small frame house that was almost buried under a broad snowdrift deposited by the prevailing northeasterly gales. On one side a trough dug through the snow led to a small door that opened into a very low hallway. A second door at the far end of the hallway gave entry to the single large room in which the family of Kuvlu lived.

The dawn light was still too faint to be seen through the small window in the east wall of the house, but the dogs' spirited howling had awakened an old man, Sakiak, father of Kuvlu. He knew despite the darkness that it was morning, so he lay on his side, head braced on one hand, waiting for the sleepiness to leave him. No one else had awakened. He could barely make out a large bed near the south window where Kuvlu, his wife Nuna, and two of their smaller children slept. Three more children occupied another bed, and an older son, Patik, used a small mattress on the floor. Sakiak, whose wife had died many years earlier, also slept on the floor.

He could hear a breeze blowing gently in the stovepipe, and he hoped it would grow no stronger. Some mornings the house rumbled and shook as if there were an earthquake, but it was only *nigiqpak*, the northeaster, which howled across the tundra so often at this season. If the wind remained light today, Sakiak would go far out onto the ocean ice to hunt.

He felt around near his bed until he found a match, which he struck against the wall and used to light a kerosene lamp. The flame caught quickly, and yellow light filled the room, which was dingy and unpainted, cluttered everywhere with the necessities of life. In addition to the beds there were several chairs and box stools, a table, containers filled with clothing, and a large iron-topped stove. Sakiak pulled several chunks of seal blubber from a box, put them into the stove, and let the glowing embers set them afire. The blubber sputtered and burned with a hot, smoky flame that quickly drove the chill from the house.

Nuna slipped out of bed, set a kettle of water on the stove, and picked up a caribou skin she had begun scraping the day before. "Perhaps you will hunt," she said in a low voice, as if she were talking to herself. "It is possible," he answered. Men were usually indefinite when they spoke of hunting, because the fickle moods of weather and ice too often mocked their plans. Sakiak ate cold slices of boiled caribou meat left from the night before, dipping each one into a saucer of fermented seal oil to give it flavor. When he finished, he drank the cup of strong coffee that Nuna had set before him.

She used the remaining hot water to make a pot of black tea, which she poured into a battered thermos. Sakiak slipped the thermos into a cylindrical pouch made from caribou hide with the thick fur inside. This pouch would help keep the tea hot, since a thermos alone was inadequate when the temperature was far below zero. He packed the thermos, a few biscuits, and a small frozen fish into an oblong sealskin bag that he always carried when he hunted. The bag also contained binoculars, an ammunition pouch, matches, a sewing kit, and a seal-pulling harness.

Sakiak opened the door and stepped into the dark hallway. Supercooled air rushed into the house, condensing instantly to a thick cloud of steam that spread along the floor. He returned in a moment, carrying a voluminous bundle of clothing, all made from caribou hide. Two of the children, who had awakened, sat quietly watching as he pulled a pair of bulky fur pants over his cloth trousers. He slipped his feet into fur-lined inner boots and tugged his outer boots over them. Then he put on two wool shirts, a nylon jacket, and a knit watch cap. Over it all he pulled a bulky parka, its fur turned inside and white cloth covering the scraped skin outside.

The caribou hide clothing was light and comfortable, but its loose fit and thick fur made Sakiak look almost twice his normal size. A ruff of stiff-haired wolverine fur encircled his wrinkled face. He smiled at the children and gave one of them a pinch with his stumpy, leather-skinned fingers before turning to leave. On the way to the door he picked up his hunting bag, gloves, and fur mittens.

Moments later he emerged from the long hallway, now carrying a rifle in a homemade sheath of white canvas. He straightened up outside the door, peering into the early twilight. Needles of cold stung his face, and each time he drew breath a deep minty chill spread down his throat into his chest. "*Alapuu!*" he spoke to himself. "Cold!" It was thirty-five below zero, with a gentle breeze from the east lending added chill to the air. He pulled his gloves on before his fingers numbed but stuffed his mittens into the sealskin hunting bag. His hands would perspire if he wore mittens during the long walk out onto the ice.

Sakiak stood atop the hard drift beside Kuvlu's house. The moon was low above the northern horizon, its white profile drawn sharp against the deep black sky. Millions of stars stippled the heavens, each one standing out clear and unwavering. These were good signs. If the horizon was hazy and the stars twinkled erratically, it forewarned of a gale that could crack and move the sea ice. Looking southeastward, Sakiak saw the black sky lighten to pale blue. Gold streaks flowed upward from the invisible sun, illuminating a few wisps of high cloud. If the east wind held, he thought, tomorrow would be bitter cold. But this was a good day to hunt.

He turned and walked along a hard-packed sled trail that led to the edge of the village and onto the frozen ocean. There were lights in several houses now, but Sakiak was the first man out to begin his day's activities. Only the dogs watched him pass, aroused by the noisy squeaking of snow beneath his steps. He was careful to stay clear of the chain-tethered animals, knowing they might lunge at any stranger who passed within reach. Some dogs stood up to bark or growl as he walked by. Most, however, remained in a tight curl on the snow, breathing into the thick bushes of their tails and conserving the warmth of their bodies.

Beyond the last house, the trail followed a gently sloping ravine that opened onto the snow-covered beach. The trail split at the ocean's edge, one fork going north along the coast and the other heading out onto the sea ice. Sakiak chose the seaward trail. He walked with short, brisk steps, rather stiff-legged and somewhat bent at the waist. His hunting bag and rifle were slung horizontally on his back, each suspended from a strap that passed across his chest and shoulders. He carried a long iron-pointed staff, or *unaaq*, that he would use primarily for jabbing the ice to test its safety.

■ ■ ■

For the first half-mile the ice was almost perfectly flat, except for a few low hummocks, or ice piles, where the floes had moved and been crushed the previous fall. The surface was also punctuated by the minor undulations of snowdrifts, packed hard as a wooden floor by the pounding winds. Sakiak's practiced eye could tell which drifts had been shaped by the cold northeasters and which by the warmer south winds. If fog or a blinding snowstorm caught him, he would navigate by watching, or even feeling, the configuration of the drifts.

Shortly, he reached the first high ridges of piled ice. He picked his way up the side of a huge mountain of tumbled slabs and boulders, from which he could look far out over the pack. When he stood at the top, he scanned the vast expanse of snow-covered ice that stretched beyond him. It was still gray twilight, but in the crystal air and brightness of snow the sea ice stood out sharply to the distant horizon. From his lofty perch, Sakiak looked over an environment that appeared totally chaotic and forbidding. Huge ice piles and ridges interlaced the surface everywhere, encircling countless small flat areas and occasionally fringing a broad plain of unbroken ice.

To the unpracticed eye this jumbled seascape would have seemed utterly impenetrable and unattractive. But to the Eskimo it held a different promise. He would find an easy trail by weaving among the hummocks, crossing them at low places. And he would find his prey, the seal, that now swam in dark waters beneath the pavement of ice. For although this world appeared silent and lifeless, the sea below was rich with living things. The currents carried millions of tiny planktonic organisms, the basis of a long chain of biological interrelationships. Larger invertebrates and fish fed upon the drifting clouds of krill, and they in turn fell prey to warm-blooded animals that rose to the surface for air. Seals lived all winter among the congealing floes, gnawing and scratching holes through the ice to reach the air above or rising in the steaming cracks. And, on the ice surface, polar bears and Eskimos stalked the seals.

Sakiak searched the pack with is binoculars, their cold eyepieces stinging his skin. He was attentive to minute details, hoping to pick out the yellowish color of a polar bear's fur against the whiteness of the snow. He looked also for the fresh black lines of cracks and for rising clouds of steam that would mark open holes and leads. Long minutes passed before he took the binoculars from his eyes, satisfied that there were no bears or open places in the area. The ice was packed firm against the coast and would not move today unless the wind or current changed. It was a perfect time for an old man to wait for a seal at its breathing hole.

In a moment Sakiak was down from the ice pile, walking seaward again along the sled trail. About a mile out from the coast he passed the frozen carcasses of two old dogs, half-covered by blown snow. They had been shot early in the winter by their owner, who was replacing them with strong pups. This fate awaited all dogs that outlived their usefulness, for though Eskimos appreciated their animals they could ill afford the luxury of emotional attachment to them. Sakiak had used dogs all his life, but like all the older hunters he often preferred to walk. Animals frequently saw or heard a dog team long before they could detect a lone man afoot, so it was better to hunt this way. If the kill was heavy, a man could drag part of it home and return with a team for the rest.

The trail wound and twisted across the ice, which made it long but relatively smooth. Still, it crossed many ridges that the Eskimos had laboriously chopped and smoothed to make the passage as easy as possible. About two miles out the trail entered a field of very rough ice, with some ridges forty to sixty feet high. Broad slabs of ice four feet thick had been tossed on end and pushed into the air like huge monuments that towered high above a man's head. The far edge of this rough area was marked by a single ridge that stretched unbroken for miles, its direction generally paralleling the distant coast. The outer face was a sheer wall of pulverized ice, ground flat and smooth by the motion of the pack.

Sakiak sat down to rest and cool off beside this ridge. His long walk had generated too much warmth, and if he did not stop he would begin to perspire. He knew that moisture robbed clothing of its warmth, so he always tempered his labors during these cold months to avoid overheating. The long ridge where Sakiak rested marked the outermost edge of the landfast floe, an immobile apron of ice that extended far out from the land. An early winter gale had driven the ice against the coast and caused it to pile so high and deep that the entire floe had become solidly anchored to the bottom of the ocean. The ice beyond it was the mobile Arctic pack, which moved according to the dictates of current and wind.

Hunters knew that landfast ice rarely moved during the winter unless a tremendous gale arose, with an accompanying high tide that lifted the ice free of the bottom. Landfast ice meant safety because it would not drift away, carrying men out to sea with it. But the pack was different. Hunters who ventured onto it were suspicious and watchful, constantly checking wind and current to be sure the ice would not break away from the landfast floe. If this happened, and it sometimes did, they would be stranded beyond a widening lead, an open crack that blocked their return to shore. Men who drifted away often died without seeing land again.

A week earlier, powerful onshore winds had driven the pack against the landfast ice, where it had remained without moving ever since. Sakiak would now decide if it was safe to go beyond the final grounded ridge. He walked along its edge until he found a narrow crack covered with dark, thin ice. With the point of his *unaaq*, he chiseled a fair-sized hole through it. Then he cut a bit of sealskin thong from his boot tie, chewed it until it was moist, and dropped it into the black water. The white thong sank slowly downward until it cleared the bottom edge of the ice, then drifted off eastward, toward the land. Finally it was enveloped in the blackness.

Sakiak stood up and looked out onto the pack. The current flowed from the west, from the sea toward the land, gently but with enough force to hold the ice ashore against opposing pressure from the easterly breeze. He had studied the movements of ice throughout his life, and he remembered well the lessons taught him by old hunters during his youth. With this knowledge and experience he could judge to near perfection the mood of the pack. Today it would be safe, so long as the wind and current pushed against each other. He would look for breathing holes somewhere not far from the landfast ice, where he could scurry to safety if conditions changed. Old men knew there was no point in taking chances. "The ice is like a mean dog," they warned. "He waits for you to stop watching, and then he tries to get you."

Sakiak climbed to the top of a nearby ridge and scanned the pack with his binoculars. Jagged lines of hummocks pierced sharply into the brightening sky. The day was now full and blue, brilliant refracted twilight glowing high above the seaward horizon. He smiled as he squinted into the brightness. Indeed, it was *Siqinyasaq tatqiq*, "moon of the returning sun." But the cold needling his cheekbones reminded him that it was still midwinter, and that he must work fast to hunt before darkness closed over the sky again.

He saw no hint of life on the pack, but the configurations of ice told him where best to look for it. Just beyond a low ridge several hundred yards away there was a long plain of flat ice, its color and lack of snow cover indicating that it was not more than three feet thick. This would be an ideal place to search for the breathing holes of seals, because they were easy to see on such ice. The sled trail had ended at the edge of landfast ice, so he picked out an easy route before heading toward the flat. Younger hunters often failed to reconnoiter in this way, considering it a waste of time. But instead of moving faster they were forced to clamber laboriously over the rough ice, and they often came home bruised and exhausted.

It was not long before Sakiak stood at the edge of the big flat. Its surface was completely free of snow but was covered everywhere with large, fluffy crystals of frost, some so thin and feathery that they shivered in the breeze. They were made flexible by salty moisture from the ice, which prevented them from freezing hard, and when Sakiak walked on the frost his tracks were slushy despite the intense cold. This was why ice hunters wore boots soled with waterproof seal hide, which kept their feet dry on the moist surface.

He moved quickly along one side of the flat, searching for the telltale signs of a breathing hole. Presently he stopped, looking at the ice nearby. He saw a little group of thin ice chunks frozen into the surface, scattered in a circle about a handbreadth in diameter. When this ice was newly formed, a seal had broken up through it to breathe, leaving a small opening with bits of ice around it. The hole was never used again, but this frozen scar remained.

If the seal had continued to use such a hole as the ice thickened, it would have looked quite different. Each time the animal returned, water would slosh out over the ice and freeze, eventually building up a small, irregularly shaped dome with a little hole in its top. By scratching and gnawing, the seal kept this dome hollow inside, like a miniature igloo. Beneath this structure the hole widened into a tunnel through the ice, large enough to accommodate the seal's body when it came up to breathe. The Eskimos called such breathing holes *allus*.

Sakiak walked to the far end of the flat without seeing an *allu* or even another scar. So he turned back, following a low ridge that flanked the opposite side. He had not gone far when he spotted an *allu* just a few yards from the base of the ridge. It was very large and nearly cone-shaped, so he knew at a glance that it had been made by the huge *uguruk*, or bearded seal. He bent low, stiff-legged, moving his trunk from side to side and peering into its opening. The interior was very dim, but he could make out its round entryway, covered by a layer of dark gray ice. This was a disappointing find. The ice was almost a day old, indicating that the seal was not using this *allu* often.

If the days were longer he might wait there, for a bearded seal was a fine catch indeed. But with few hours of daylight he needed a hole that was visited more frequently. He would remember this *allu*, and if the ice did not move he might check it again to see if the seal returned. Sakiak memorized the shape of the ridge nearby so he could easily guide himself to this spot another day.

Breathing holes were often somewhat clustered, so he looked carefully around the area. Seeing none, he climbed the ridge to inspect a small flat on its opposite side. He was surprised to find that the flat was cut by a broad crack, perhaps ten yards across, covered with newly frozen ice. The crack, which must have opened during the past week's storm, made a jagged swath across the flat and sliced cleanly through a ridge on its far side. Sakiak marveled at the power of moving ice, which could split a heavy ridge into two sections as a man would cut through blubber with his knife. The crack probably ran for miles, and there would almost certainly be a few breathing holes in its covering of young ice. It also offered Sakiak an easy trail through the hummocky areas.

Sakiak made his way down the ridge and onto the frozen crack. He followed it across the flat, through the chasm of the split ridge, and onto another flat. There he saw what he was looking for. Almost in the middle of the crack was a nearly perfect little dome, the *allu* of a ringed seal, or *natchiq*. He peered closely into its opening and saw deep black inside. "It's good," he murmured softly to himself. The blackness was a circle of open water with a transparent skin of new ice forming at its edges, just a few inches below the quarter-sized opening of the *allu*. Not an hour before, while Sakiak walked out across the landfast ice, a seal had risen here to breathe.

There was no time to waste. For all he knew, the animal might be heading for this hole now, and he was not ready for it. He slipped off his hunting bag and rifle, laying them on the ice together with his *unaaq*. Then he went quickly to the nearest hummock and kicked free two blocks of ice for a stool and footrest. After carrying them back, he again inspected the interior of the *allu*. Its opening was slightly off center, and the tunnel appeared to angle somewhat away from the vertical. From this Sakiak knew which direction the seal would face when it came to breathe, and he would angle his rifle slightly for the deadliest possible shot.

Now he placed the two ice blocks about a foot from the hole, along its southeast side. He calculated automatically, almost without thought, the effects of wind and light. There was enough brightness to create a faint shadow, which must not fall across the hole. And he must not sit upwind lest the seal be frightened by his scent. He also preferred to face away from the biting chill of the breeze. He emptied his hunting bag onto the thick ice alongside the crack and pulled his rifle from its canvas sheath. The bag would insulate and cushion his stool while the sheath insulated the footrest. Eskimos always took pains to minimize loss of heat from their bodies in every way possible, and Sakiak knew the wait would be a cold one even in the best circumstances.

He placed his *unaaq* on the thick ice, where its shadow would not be visible from below, and he adjusted the ice blocks so they could not jiggle or squeak noisily. Then he sat down on one block and put his feet on the other, so that his legs were held straight out before him, Eskimo fashion. He could sit this way for many hours without tiring. When he was seated atop the ice blocks, his menacing presence could not be detected by a seal looking up through the glowing translucence of the gray ice.

The bolt of his rifle clicked loudly in the brittle cold as he thrust a shell into the chamber. Then he placed the weapon crosswise over the tops of his boots, where it was least likely to compress his clothing and cause chilling. Its muzzle faced the *allu* but did not hang over where the seal might see it. He had taken the precaution of standing a flat chip of ice alongside the little opening to screen his intrusive shape from the seal's eyes as it rose to breathe.

Now he would wait.

· · ·

It was impossible to know when the seal would appear. In fifty winters of hunting at breathing holes, Sakiak had learned not to think too much of time. It might be fifteen minutes, perhaps an hour. Perhaps many hours. Sometimes the animal never returned.

Sakiak knew of old men who, in times of starvation, had waited beside an *allu* for twenty-four hours. Nowadays the young men refused to hunt at breathing holes, preferring to wait until a wide crack or lead formed so they could shoot seals in the open water. When Sakiak was a boy the men had relied upon harpoons, which could not be thrown far enough to strike a seal swimming freely out in a lead. But a harpoon was as good as a rifle for hunting at breathing holes, perhaps better. When a seal was harpooned, a line attached to the point ensured that the animal would not sink or be carried away by the current.

Young men said that breathing-hole hunting was too cold, that it involved too much waiting. The old men said only that people must eat. They had learned the art of enduring patience, as if they could merge their thoughts with the timeless physical world that surrounded them. Life, after all, was a game of waiting. One could not expect that the weather, ice, and animals would do a man's bidding. If a man would live, he must persist, wait, endure.

Sakiak was enveloped in still silence, interrupted only by the occasional buffeting of wind against his parka hood. His breath condensed on the ruff around his face and on his scraggly moustache, coating each hair with thick white frost. He could feel the immensity of the pack surrounding him, its quiet, latent power.

Radiant amber flowed up the wall of the sky before him, hinting of warmth in some distant world, while the pervasive cold drew closer around his body. Time faded away to a dim consciousness at the core of the hunter's mind.

Twilight grew and spread slowly southward, then edged toward the west. The fullest light of midday came, then imperceptibly began to fade. Sakiak drew his arms from the sleeves of his parka and held them against his body for warmth. He was shivering. Frost had collected on his eyelashes and brows. Occasionally he poked a bare hand up through the neck of his parka and held it against his cheek to warm the stiff, numb flesh. His toes felt large and icy cold. Perhaps the temperature was falling, he thought. Indeed, it was now minus forty, but the wind was fading as it grew colder.

Sakiak wished he had brought the boy along. His grandson Patik was old enough to hunt and could make the seal come to the *allu* where he waited. If he walked in a broad circle around Sakiak, he would frighten the seal away from its other holes and force it toward the hunter's station. Had the ice been perfectly smooth, Sakiak could have accomplished this alone by finding every breathing hole in the area and urinating on it. The powerful scent would frighten the seal away, leaving it only the hunted *allu* to use. It was funny to think how a seal must plunge away in frightened surprise when it smelled urine in its *allu*. But in rough ice many breathing holes were concealed in open spaces beneath hummocks and snowdrifts, where a man could never find them.

Almost two hours had passed. A growing ache spread up Sakiak's legs and back, but he dared not move to relieve the discomfort. The seal might be near enough to hear any noise transmitted through the ice to the water below. So he moved only his head and arms, even then very carefully.

It was also important to watch the surrounding ice in case a polar bear happened to approach him. Bears would occasionally stalk a man, if they were so thin and hungry that starvation drove fear out of them. But today it seemed there was no life anywhere, except for the silent lives beneath the pack. Sakiak wondered how deep the water under him might be. And he thought the current could soon shift and flow from the east, as it always did when intensely cold air moved in off the great expanse of land that stretched eastward away from the coast.

He was now shivering hard, and he wondered if his shaking might jiggle the ice stool, making a noise that would scare away the seals. He smiled, thinking what a great joke that would be after such a long, cold wait!

But beneath him at that moment a seal torpedoed through the black-gray water, darting and arcing in pursuit of the fleeting silver of fishes. It dodged between the blue and emerald-green walls of ice protruding downward beneath the hummocks. Huge inverted ice mountains blocked its path, but it sensed them and turned away before striking invisible barriers deep in the blackness.

In the freedom of its dense medium, the seal could ignore the encumbrances of gravity. It swam on its side, then upside down, then coasted to a stop in midwater. There it hung quietly in the dark silence, drifting slowly with the current, like a footloose star in the vastness of space. But this space was far from an empty void. Nervous shoals of fish left glowing trails as they spun and needled through luminescent plankton. Tiny jellyfish pulsed and parachuted, trailing delicate streamers beneath them. And, far below, crabs littered the bottom, waiting for those above to die and become their food.

For more than a minute the seal remained motionless, ignoring the fish that swam too near. It was in need of air and was listening. Then it suddenly whirled and shot upward toward a circle of white that glimmered faintly in the high distance.

When it reached the underside of the ice, the seal turned slowly beneath the circle. It hesitated a moment, then swam slowly upward into the narrow passage. Reaching the surface, it poked its nose out for an instant, sampling the air, then dropped again. The air was fresh and stinging of cold. It rose again, emerging into the bright igloo of ice, globed eyes wide and black, nostrils flaring and closing.

· · ·

In the silence of the pack, after a long wait, the seal's approach was startling and exciting. Sakiak first heard, almost sensed without hearing, a pulsation of the water inside the *allu*. Then he saw water flow through the opening and over the ice outside, where it instantly froze to a fresh glaze. This water was forced up ahead of the seal as it rose from below.

Sakiak heard scratching as the seal cleared away newly formed ice at the tunnel's upper opening. He quickly slipped his arms into the sleeves of his parka, then remained perfectly still. The cold had vanished. Shivering ceased as warmth spread from mind to muscle.

He fixed his eyes on the *allu*, consumed with intense concentration. His lips moved slightly, almost imperceptibly. "Come seal," he whispered, asking the animal to give itself to him. "Come. . . ." It was only a thought this time.

In a moment the seal obeyed Sakiak's will. It took a first short, hissing breath, smelling the air for signs of danger. He did not move. He expected the brief silence that followed, knowing the next breath would be a deep one.

Whoosh!

It was a long, drawn-out hiss that sent a misty spray from the opening. This noise was loud enough to drown out the sound of Sakiak's movement as he reached down and picked up his rifle from his legs. He was careful to spread his arms so his clothing would not scrape noisily, and he was still before the deep breath was finished.

Whoosh!

Again the animal breathed. Sakiak lifted his rifle and held it vertical, with the thumb of his upper hand against the trigger. Again he waited, as the second breath stopped.

Whoosh!

On the third breath he moved his rifle straight above the *allu*, its muzzle inches from the opening. His face was expressionless. His resolve was complete. Without a second's hesitation, he deliberately squeezed the trigger.

For the seal, breath cut short. A sudden *crack!* only half heard before the world was shut out in closing clouds of black.

For the hunter, a sudden deafening explosion. The *allu* split and shattered. Fragments of ice dyed crimson. The seal bobbing on the pulse of water, grotesque and broken, instantly detached from the reality of life.

Sakiak ran to fetch his *unaaq*. Using its sharp point, he chipped the rest of the *allu* away, then snagged the animal with the metal hook on its other end. The seal was still quivering, so he held it until movement stopped. With the knife he carried on his belt he slit the skin of its upper lip, then he pushed the loop end of his seal-pulling harness through this cut and fastened it around the animal's nose.

This done, Sakiak held the line under one foot while he chiseled the hole until it was large enough so he could pull out the seal. If he had not secured the seal quickly with a line, it might have been carried off by the current. In thicker ice, where the seal would enter though a long, cigar-shaped tunnel, this would be unnecessary; winter-killed seals were buoyant from their thick layer of blubber, so they would float well up into the tunnel where the current count not take them away.

Finally, Sakiak pulled the seal out onto the ice. It was completely limp and flexible, like a sack full of liquid. Blood flowed and coagulated on its skin, freezing in thick layers around the wound. It was large for a ringed seal, about four feet long and weighing perhaps a hundred pounds. And its hide was deep black, patterned with small whitish circlets. The *Inupiat* called a dark seal like this *magamnasik*.

• • •

The warmth of excitement that had flared inside Sakiak died quickly, and he found himself shivering again. Before starting back he should eat something and drink the hot tea in his thermos. Eskimos knew that food kindled heat inside a man's body, so it was important to eat well and often during the cold hunts. Heavy steam billowed from the thermos when he opened it. He drank quickly, feeling the hot liquid flow down his throat to the cold pit of his stomach. Refreshed, he took the hard-frozen fish he had brought along and peeled off its skin. Then he cut it into small sections and hungrily ate the raw chunks. Its oily fat would bring him quick warmth and energy.

More hot tea and a couple of frozen biscuits finished his meal. When he had drunk his fill of tea he spilled the remainder out onto the snow, staining its white surface yellow brown. It made sharp, crackling noises as it immediately froze to a brittle crust. He felt deep appreciation for the food and for the seal he had killed. He could remember his grandfather chanting thanks to an abiding spirit that helped him, but Sakiak thanked the Christian God with a short prayer in Eskimo.

He rested for a few minutes, looking at the distant sky. The light was fading, and he had a long walk before him. Perhaps in a few days he would return to this *allu*. Often several animals used one hole, and they might eventually come back in spite of the damage done to it. But now there was little time to waste. Sakiak lighted a cigarette and put his equipment back into the hunting bag. When this was finished he took his knife and made a long slit down the seal's belly. Then he cut a wide slab of blubber from the abdomen and both flanks, laying it aside on the ice. Along each side of the slit he made a series of holes in the hide, and through these he laced a piece of heavy cord, sewing the animal back together. Removing the blubber made it almost ten pounds lighter, and ten pounds would make a noticeable difference to an old man pulling a large seal home over the ice.

Now he slung his hunting bag and rifle case across his back, placed the strap of his seal-pulling harness around his chest, and began walking toward the landfast ice. The limp seal, still warm inside, slid along easily behind him. Sakiak had pulled hundreds of seals this way, however, and he knew that its weight would grow as he crossed the piled ice.

Once, when he was young and strong, Sakiak had shot two bearded seals weighing several hundred pounds apiece and decided to pull both of them home. He cut every bit of meat from one animal, discarding the bones, skin and entrails. Then he removed the entrails of the other, stuffed the meat of the first seal into the empty carcass, and sewed the skin back together. The load was still very heavy, and he had pulled late into the night before reaching the settlement, completely exhausted.

Thinking of that experience seemed to lighten his load, and soon he could see the edge of the landfast ice. This was good, because he wanted to be off the pack while there was still fair light. He was taking a long route, because by weaving back and forth he could stay almost entirely on flat ice. In spite of the deep cold he soon became overheated from pulling, and so he decided to rest at the base of a small ridge.

He was about to sit down on a large ice boulder when he noticed what appeared to be an *allu* in the flat ice some distance away. Curious, and hoping to find a place to hunt another day, he walked quickly to it, leaving the seal behind. Even before he reached it he could tell that something was wrong. The little dome was partially caved in, and along one side the ice had been dug away. He knew immediately what had happened. "Ah, *nanuq!*" he whispered. Wandering away from the hole was a set of broad footprints, the track of a polar bear. It was not fresh. A haze of frost crystals already filled the prints, showing that a day had passed since they were made.

Sakiak inspected the tracks again and again, looking off in the direction they faced. The bear had hunted at this *allu* and, like him, had found success. It first dug around the dome until the ice was very thin. Then it filled the excavated area with snow scraped from the ice, so the seal could detect no change as it came up inside. Finishing this, it stood beside the *allu* at a right angle to the wind, awaiting the seal's return. Eventually, perhaps many hours later, the bear heard its prey breathing within the dome. In an instant it smashed the surrounding ice with both paws, simultaneously crushing the animal's skull. Then it pulled the seal out onto the ice, squeezing it though a hole so small that many bones broke inside the lifeless body. So it was that Eskimo and polar bear hunted the same animal in almost the same way.

The hole was now frozen over. Flecks of blood spotted the bear's tracks, showing that it had carried the seal away to eat it elsewhere. Sometimes bears slept long and soundly in the rough ice near a kill site, digesting the meal before moving on. Sakiak saw darkness moving up the eastern sky and looked away along the tracks. The bear might be somewhere nearby, or it might be far away over the ice horizon. From the age of the tracks he suspected it had moved on, but he would follow them for a short distance to look for more signs.

Several hundred yards away, near a broad field of rough ice, he found the seal's carcass. The bear had eaten only its skin and blubber, leaving the rest behind to be gnawed by the little white foxes that so often followed bears. They had already eaten half the meat, showing that many hours had passed since the bear's meal. The bear must have been fat and in its prime; otherwise it could not afford to eat only the choicest parts. Sakiak was sure now that it was far away, but he climbed a ridge and scanned the surrounding floes for a long time to be sure. Seeing nothing, he returned to his seal and resumed his trek toward the landfast ice.

Now he was careful to look behind him every few minutes, to be sure no bear was following. Bears often followed a man's trail over the sea ice, especially if it was scented with the blood and oil of a seal. Sakiak knew men who had felt a tug on their seal-pulling harness as they dragged their catch home in the dim hours of the evening. They turned to see a white bear, ready to stake claim to the animal. Old-timers often warned the young hunters to slip out of the harness quickly and grab for their rifles if ever they felt something strange while pulling a seal.

A man named Takirak, who lived in the neighboring village of Utqeavik, had an unexpected encounter with a bear when Sakiak was still a boy. He was setting fox traps on the landfast ice and carried only a long knife. A skinny bear appeared nearby, looking as if it might attack him. Takirak was a brave man who knew much of animals, so he handled the bear wisely. He drew his knife and walked threateningly toward it, speaking in a firm, low voice. "Go away, bear, or I will cut up your handsome face." The animal backed away, but it persisted in following as Takirak walked homeward. Each time it came too near, he threatened it again. Finally, when they drew within earshot of the village's howling dogs, the bear ran off and did not return.

■ ■ ■

It was not long before Sakiak reached the ridge that marked the edge of landfast ice. He followed it southward until he found the sled trail, and there he rested briefly before heading landward. Twilight was fading rapidly now, and distant ridges loomed mysteriously in the growing gloom of evening. The trail crossed many low ridges, and Sakiak found himself becoming warm and a little tired. Fortunately the snow had been pounded slick by the passage of many dog teams over the previous months, so the carcass slid along easily. In any case, old men, like old dogs, were tough and long-winded. The young were faster and had more brute power, but they often tired long before their elders.

Sakiak thought of these things as he trudged across the silent floes. He was alone, one small old man on the vastness of an ice-covered sea. The breeze had died away to an occasional puff, and his footsteps squeaked loudly in the steel-hard cold. Beads of perspiration covered his forehead, just inches from the rime of thick frost that whitened his parka ruff. He melted ice droplets from the long whiskers of his moustache by holding his tongue against them, refreshing himself with the cold moisture. Ahead he could see the village, sharp and black against the snow-covered tundra that swept away to meet the sky. Smoke from the chimneys rose, then flattened out in a thick haze that hung over the houses.

Soon he was crossing the last stretches of flat ice that fringed the shore. It had been a long, slow walk from the edge of the landfast floe, and Sakiak thought fondly of the comfort that awaited him. Nuna would have hot tea ready, and stew made from caribou meat. Behind him the last streaks of flaming gold spread widely along the sea horizon beneath the overarching blackness of night.

He could see a dog team returning home amid a chorus of envious howls and challenging barks from tethered animals. Someone was hauling in large blocks of freshwater ice cut from a tundra lake near the village. He wondered if any hunters had killed caribou today far inland where tall willows broke the sweeping wind. Fresh tongue and heart, boiled together in a large pot, would await the families of the lucky ones.

Sakiak walked slowly up the ravine that ended atop the bank and followed the trail toward Kuvlu's house. Children of all sizes ran out to walk beside him, asking endless admiring questions. "Where did you catch the seal?" "Did you see a bear?" "Will you eat the seal's boiled intestines tonight?" Sakiak said little, letting the older children invent answers for him. He loved to hear the laughter of children and was always happy when they ran to meet him. Someday, perhaps, they would hunt to feed him when he no longer walked out over the ice.

Migalik, a young man, was feeding his dogs when Sakiak passed. "Ah, Sakiak, you have killed a seal. *Azahaa*, you're a man!"

"And you," he answered, "perhaps you have traveled today." Migalik said he had gone far south along the coast, nearly to Qayaqsirvik, searching for polar bears. But he saw nothing except a few wolverine tracks and a fox caught in one of Nauruk's traps. The two men talked briefly, their conversation raptly followed by several young boys who wished they could hunt instead of spending their days inside the village school. Some of the boys had already killed their first animals and passed the meat out among the old people to ensure luck as they grew to manhood.

When the men had told each other the events of their day's hunting, Sakiak pulled his seal the rest of the way home. His grandchildren, bundled in parkas that were miniature replicas of his own, ran out from the house to meet him. He joked briefly with them, then told the oldest boy to pull the seal in for his mother to skin and butcher. When she finished, he was to carry a piece of its meat to Saatuk, the old woman who lived in a sod hut at the far end of the village.

■ ■ ■

Sakiak stood looking out over the sea ice. He wondered about the bear whose tracks he had followed. It was a big one, with meat that would drip with fat and a pelt that might bring a handsome price indeed. He did not think about killing it, lest he bring bad luck upon himself. Tomorrow would be very cold and still, perhaps so cold it would be wise to stay at home. But he would like to walk out and look for the bear.

The moon, enormous and brilliant white, was lifting itself into the southern sky. Long gray shadows stretched out over the snow. The sea ice emerged again from darkness, looking distant and utterly detached from the world of the land. Sakiak brushed a shower of sparkling frost crystals from the ruff of his parka, turned, and disappeared into the long hallway of the house.

TREAT IT RIGHT
SCOTT McMILLION

For those of us who love the call of remote backcountry, the idea of hiking or canoeing and camping in country that grizzly bears and wolves call home is an experience that takes us to the outer limits of outdoor adventure. Even in the black bear country of the Canadian bush, precautions must be taken with food and campsites. And while black bears can be troublesome, even frightening, and sometimes have killed people, they are not in the same league with the grizzly in attacks on humans. In grizzly country, food must be stored high and away from your sleeping tent. Your presence on the trail must be obvious, with the use of bells or even your voice to alert bears and hopefully send them fleeing. Encounters with sows with cubs must be avoided at all costs. A spray can of bear repellent, within easy reach, is a good idea in areas known to harbor grizzlies. In places like Yellowstone and Glacier National Parks, bear warnings are posted, and sometimes entire trails and campsites are closed. Even when you apply all these precautions, there is still a possibility that you may experience a seriously bad grizzly encounter. A remote possibility, yes, but it's there. In his wonderful book Mark of the Grizzly, *Scott McMillion shows us how things can go wrong in bear country, how we can help them go right, and how respect for the grizzly and its range is critical to the bear's survival.*

■ ■ ■

Put yourself in Buck Wilde's shoes.

You're hiking alone in Glacier National Park in Montana when you find a blue hat lying in a trail. Then you spot a camera on a tripod, laid carefully down, the tripod legs neatly folded, the lens cap on. There's a small red backpack there, too, and this makes you suspicious and curious and you start to pay some serious attention. You move thirty feet or so back the way you came and there about three feet into the brush you spot the bad news: a pool of blood, a foot or more wide and still fresh.

Then you notice more blood, spots of it leading down the trail, and you see some grizzly bear tracks, claw marks scratched into the hard-packed ground. You follow them, making plenty of noise and moving downhill very slowly for about five hundred feet, until you find a bunch of scuff marks on the trail, a place where something heavy has been swept back and forth a few times. You keep going and you find more blood, then little pieces of what must be human flesh. You find some coins, you find a bootlace, you find more blood. Puddles of it, and a blood trail leading into the woods. You have spent a lot of time around bears, and you know how dangerous they can be, but you also know they rarely kill people. Somebody is hurt very badly and the blood trail is there and you have only a can of pepper spray with you and you know somebody will surely die if you don't help so you go into the brush, where you find more coins and a wristwatch and a boot, and then you find a man lying on his left side.

The man is bitten and clawed from head to toe and the bear has eaten the meat from one arm and one buttock but his body is warm and he might still be alive even though you can't find a pulse and still there is nobody here but you and this dead or dying man. Surely you can do something, so you hustle back to the red backpack only a few hundred feet and get a coat to cover him and keep him warm, and when you get back to him after maybe five minutes the man is gone.

Not just dead. Gone.

Smears of blood tell you the bear has come back, probably after watching you follow its tracks, and has taken the man away, so you follow this grisly trail for a few steps and you see that it leads into a patch of timber so thick that you can't see anything at all.

Put yourself in Buck Wilde's shoes.

What are you going to do?

. . .

"That's when I knew I had really been more foolish than I thought I was being," Wilde recalls of that day, the third of October 1992, a sunny Saturday in the high country. "I had the pepper spray in my hand the whole time, with the safety off. I was scared shitless. That was the point when I made the decision that I was in over my head and I had to get out. It was time to think about myself and other people, who I knew were alive."

Wilde was just off the Loop Trail, a steep and vigorous four-mile hike that leads from the Going-to-the-Sun Road to the Granite Park Chalet, a popular backcountry destination. But it was late in the season—the first days of October can be the early part of winter in some years—and as far as Wilde knew, there wasn't another person around for miles. Still, it was a pleasant Saturday, only about noon, and there was a good chance that other hikers would arrive soon and walk into an ugly situation. So Wilde backtracked to the trail, walked downhill a quarter-mile, and pinned a note to the middle of the trail with a small rock.

"A man has been attacked by a bear," the note said. "Turn around and go back to the highway. Shout and make noise every hundred feet or so. Don't run, but move fast. Send help."

Wilde left his bear spray with the note and gave instructions on how to use it. Then he moved back up trail to the chalet, closed at the time, and met some other hikers who had just arrived. He sent them back to Logan Pass, a relatively flat eight-mile hike away, but a place with lots of traffic and a visitor center, the quickest source of help. He gave them a note for park rangers.

"Help," it said. "Discovered signs of bear mauling about a quarter- to a half-mile downhill from chalet backcountry campsite. Followed another quarter-mile and found body. He was in bad shape but alive. Went back to get coat to cover him and body was gone.

"Met these people at chalet. I plan to stay here for two reasons.

"1. To turn people back toward Logan Pass visitor center.

"2. To take National Park Service personnel to site I last saw victim."

He signed the note "Seriously, Buck Wilde" and asked the hikers to turn back anybody they met coming toward the chalet.

After the messengers left, Wilde left another note at a second trail intersection, then climbed to the chalet's second-story deck to settle in and wait, scanning the area with his binoculars, looking for bears and watching for any hikers who might be coming in. At one point he heard a scream somewhere down on the Loop Trail. He didn't investigate. He had already spent an hour or more too close to a grizzly bear's fresh kill. He'd already pushed his luck. Enough was enough.

· · ·

Wilde is an unusual man. Forty-three years old at the time, he had given himself his name when, at the age of forty, he gave up a lucrative career as an electrical engineer and launched a new one in wildlife photography. He spends several months a year in the wild, moving between places like Yellowstone National Park and Alaska, Florida and Southeast Asia, with periodic stays in his adopted home of Sun Valley, Idaho. It's a tough way to make a living, but he's been successful, publishing ten photo books. He lives a lifestyle he readily describes as "eccentric," one that often brings him into close contact with grizzly bears. He's been charged several times but never attacked.

Wilde had walked into the Granite Park area the previous afternoon and spent the night in the backcountry campground. There were no other campers. He hoisted his food high into the air on the food pole there, then went to bed early and slept late. He walked around the area for an hour or so after he got up in the morning, then went back to the campground to fix breakfast in the designated cooking area, which is separate from the sleeping area to keep from attracting bears to the tents.

Sometime during the meal of hot cereal and tea, he caught a quick glimpse of a small grizzly bear. He heard a woof, probably from the cub's mother, and the little bear took off running toward the Loop Trail. Wilde hastily cleaned up his breakfast and raised his gear back up on the food pole. He found fresh grizzly tracks, small ones, covering the tracks he had left less than an hour earlier, grabbed his camera, and took off in the direction he had seen the bear going. It was about half past eleven in the morning.

By then the bears probably had already attacked John Petranyi, a forty-year-old jazz buff from Madison, Wisconsin, who had hiked up the Loop Trail that morning.

"It was no more than five minutes to put the food up the pole, plus another ten to fifteen minutes to get to the point of the attack," Wilde says. "That's how quickly things unfolded there.

"In my mind, what happened was, the bears came in and saw me and smelled my food. They were looking at it but did the good bear thing and split when Mama saw one of the cubs getting too close to me and took off running down toward that trail."

Wilde knows a lot about bears, knows that grizzlies will almost always avoid an encounter with people if they have a chance. He had spent the previous summer guiding photographers to places in Alaska where they could watch, up close, as grizzlies fished for salmon. Less than a year earlier, a sow had bluff-charged him on Kodiak Island after he inadvertently came between her and one of her three cubs. She came close enough, charging from a hundred feet away, that he could feel her hot breath, and she got there fast enough that he never even had time to reach for the shotgun on the ground at his feet. That's when he decided guns weren't much good in a bear encounter, and he hasn't carried one since. He studies bear behavior, is a fanatic about keeping a clean camp, and is a self-professed "pain-in-the-ass person to go into bear country with."

"You've got to read the bear safety books. You've got to convince me you've read the books. You've got to obey the rules. And pay attention. Any time you're not, I'm giving you shit about it."

He was paying close attention as he walked toward the Loop Trail that morning, mostly because he was hoping for a good photograph. But he wasn't paying much attention to the trail itself. Rather, he was watching and listening for bears.

That's when he stumbled across Petranyi's cap, then the blood and the other grim evidence of bad trouble. That point in the trail is a narrow corridor between thickish stands of pine trees, a place where visibility reduces to twenty feet in some places. It's also where Wilde started paying even more attention.

He had walked right past the big pool of blood just off the trail, the largest amount of blood he would find, even when he finally located Petranyi. "It was pretty much his life in that pool of blood."

After that, he noticed the small spots of blood leading down the trail. Then he got to the bootlace, the coins, the place where it looked like the bear had taken the two-hundred-pound man in its mouth and shaken him, leaving the scuff marks in the trail.

Following the evidence was not something he had to force himself to do, he later said. But it wasn't easy either, and it got even harder when the blood and other sign pulled him off the trail and into the woods.

"I was spooked out of my mind, but I had every reason to believe I was alone in that situation and that this guy's life was on the line. It was a weird thing, but all my senses were heightened to the nth degree. I was hearing four times better than I normally do. And I was seeing and smelling four times better than I normally do. So I just set on the logical track and tried to do things as logically as I could. I mean I took my time.

"It wasn't like I had to force myself; it was like what had to be done. But I didn't just go whistling in there either. I mean I was scared. I looked. I observed everything. I heard everything. I continuously rotated in 360 degrees to make sure I wasn't missing something, and I made noise all the time. I expected the guy was, if not dead, then on his way to dying from the evidence I was seeing. But you don't know. I still don't know if he was actually dead when I found him."

Wilde could find no pulse, no breath. The blood around the man's wounds was turning dark when he left to get the coat.

Moving the 750 feet—rangers would later measure the distance—between the backpack and where the bear first left Petranyi's body took about fifteen minutes the first time, Wilde said, because he was moving so carefully. But he made the round-trip from Petranyi to the pack and back in about five minutes, goaded by the faint hope of trying to keep somebody alive. Moving fifteen hundred feet in five minutes is no sprint, but it's no dawdle either, especially when there's a grizzly in the area.

When he returned to the spot where the body had disappeared, there was no doubt in Wilde's mind that he was in the right place. The blood, his own tracks, and other evidence were too clear to be mistaken. Petranyi had been lying under a small tree, the only one in the area, and now he was gone.

That meant the chances that he was still clutching to life were even smaller, and Wilde knew what he had to do then: Back off, warn other people, and wait for help.

■ ■ ■

The help arrived at 5:02 p.m. in the form of a helicopter bearing two rangers armed with 12-gauge shotguns, loaded with heavy slugs. A pair of hikers had found Wilde's note on the Loop Trail (they were probably the source of the scream he had heard earlier) and hustled back to the trailhead to call rangers. The lead man in the helicopter was Charlie Logan, a Glacier veteran with long experience in managing grizzly bears.

But the rangers weren't the first ones on the scene. As Wilde waited at the chalet, scanning the hillsides and trying to control his tension, a group of four hikers arrived. They had walked in on the Highline Trail, ignoring the warnings from the people Wilde had sent that way with another note.

"They came in, like, 'Hey, let's go see that bear that killed that guy.'

"When they got in there, I was irate," Wilde recalls. "I lectured them like I probably shouldn't have. I was all over them, and they came right back at me. They said they were from Montana and live with this kind of thing all the time and wanted to see it."

The rangers were almost as disgusted with the people as Wilde was. The hikers no longer were having much fun either. They got to thinking about the bear they had seen on the hike to the chalet, and one of them asked for a ride out on the helicopter. They were in the air within moments.

. . .

It took about thirty minutes for Logan to interview Wilde and organize gear. Then the two of them, along with Ranger Curt Frain, hit the trail, hoping to find Petranyi's body before the approaching darkness fell. Stopping to inspect and photograph evidence along the way, they took twenty-four minutes to reach the body. Wilde had found Petranyi's body 175 feet from the trail. The bear had moved it another 500 feet by the time the three men found it the second time. If Wilde hadn't been there, it would have taken the rangers a lot longer to find it.

"After seeing what he had seen, it was remarkable that he offered to go back," Logan says. "It took a lot of courage."

Logan's reports described the brief trip as "challenging tracking while watching our flanks." The bear carrying Petranyi's body changed course a couple of times. Along its trail they found Petranyi's sock and bits of his shirt. Logan, a trained medic, found no evidence of life in Petranyi; the body was cold, the eyes glazed, the injuries massive.

Considering all of this and "that a real danger to us (including civilian Buck Wilde) still existed at this late hour, I decided that we quickly document and mark the scene and exit the area," Logan wrote in his reports of the incident.

Frain flagged the area and took notes while Logan stood guard, shotgun at the ready. Very fresh sign indicated the bear or bears were probably still close at hand. At this point, nobody knew for sure how many or what kind of bears were involved, but dirt had been shoved on the body, indicating the bear had claimed it as its own and was protecting it from scavengers.

The men then backtracked, continuing to photograph and document evidence, moving back to Petranyi's backpack, which they checked for food. They looked for identification, and they wanted to know if Petranyi's lunch had lured the bear. But there was no food in the pack.

That's when the bears charged.

Frain was searching the backpack "when I heard heavy, rapid pounding of feet on the trail section below us, followed by repeated woofing sounds," Logan wrote in his report. "I could not see what was running up the trail at us but guessed it was a bear so began yelling 'back bear.' Within a moment a grizzly appeared at the bend in the trail below us and stopped. I caught a glimpse of a smaller bear just behind but did not take my eyes off the larger bear, now squarely in the sights of my shotgun."

The adult bear bounced back and forth on its front paws several times, a sign of stress and agitation, looked back at its offspring, and "woofed" a few times. It was fifty feet away, measurements would show, and Logan said later that if the bear had taken one more step he would have pulled the trigger. He did not believe the bear had run upon the men by surprise, he says. It was charging.

The charge "looked like a pretty deliberate deal on the bear's part," Logan says. "But there were three of us there and we were yelling at her. I think she sized us up and decided we were too much."

Then the bears took off, but the men could still hear them, woofing and crashing in the nearby brush, tearing through the area where they had first attacked Petranyi, moving around the men in a quarter circle. By then it was getting dark fast.

Logan later would call the incident one of the biggest scares of his life, but his report is written in the deadpan style of official documents. Wilde remembers the charge a little more vividly. He says he doesn't believe that guns do much good in bear encounters, that attacks almost always happen too fast for most people to draw a weapon. But in this case Logan and Frain were ready and probably could have killed at least the sow, had they chosen to.

"We heard the bears before we saw them," Wilde says. "It was like a freight train coming up that Loop Trail, coming on full speed.

"Charlie is on the left, and [Frain] is on the right. I'm in the middle, and we're standing right on the trail. And Charlie says, 'safety off, one up in the chamber. Bead down. Start yelling.'"

So the men started yelling, "Stop bear, stop bear!" And the bears turned away.

"I don't know Charlie much outside this situation," says Wilde. "But the judgment he used right there, to not shoot those bears, I thought was very commendable. Most people would have been throwing lead. Trust me, I mean those bears were close and coming fast. But he gave them more than a fair chance, and they did enough to avoid getting shot."

Logan says he didn't shoot for a couple of reasons. First, the bear stopped when he started yelling at it. Second, he had no idea if these bears were the ones that killed Petranyi.

"I certainly didn't want to kill the wrong bear, especially one with cubs."

The men then decided, as Wilde had earlier in the day, that enough was enough. They left the pack and tripod where they lay and "cautiously retreated" to the chalet area, where Wilde broke down his camp in the increasing darkness as the rangers stood guard, shotguns at the ready.

They took Wilde to a nearby backcountry ranger station with them—he had been ready to catch what sleep he could on the second-story deck of the chalet—and spent a long, long night filling out reports, reliving the day, and trying to figure out what had happened to Petranyi. About four in the morning, they caught a couple of hours of sleep.

• • •

John Petranyi had lived a quiet life in Madison, Wisconsin, where he was a supervisor of custodians for the city government and shared a home with his father, a Hungarian immigrant. He loved jazz music, fine beers, good books, and riding his bicycle, commuting on it the six miles to his job in all kinds of weather.

But his greatest passion was getting out into wild country, according to his brother, Mark. Every year he spent his three-week vacation in the wild country of the West: climbing volcanic peaks in Oregon, exploring Alaska, mountain biking in the canyons of Utah. In 1992 he took an auto tour of the Canadian Rockies, visiting Banff, Jasper, and other national parks, camping and hiking. Glacier was the last stop on his itinerary. Had he survived the day hike to Granite Park, he would have turned toward home the next day.

"That's what he worked all year for," Mark Petranyi says. "His three-week journey into the woods."

Stocky and strong, his five foot eleven–inch frame carried almost two hundred pounds. Bicycling, jogging, and cross-country skiing kept him in good shape. He was the oldest of three sons, and his death was not the first sadness in the family: A brother had died in an accident in 1974, and his mother passed away in 1990. He was a bachelor, childless.

The evening after the day he died, a Sunday, a police chaplain came to the home of his father, also named John, and delivered the heartbreaking news. The next day, as Mark and John Senior were preparing to fly to Montana to retrieve the body, a postcard arrived at Mark's house. It was postmarked from Kalispell, just outside Glacier.

"He said he hadn't seen any bears yet but had heard they were around," Mark says. "My wife almost didn't give me the card. It was a hard one to read."

John Petranyi liked to take pictures, but he wasn't an avid wildlife photographer. Almost all of his photographs were of landscapes, Mark says, a statement backed up by the film in

John's camera, developed later by rangers. The pictures were all of the jagged peaks and cliffs that make Glacier so famous. No bears were on the film.

Mark says neither he nor his father blames the bears for John's death.

"He was just in the wrong place at the wrong time," Mark says. "It's unfortunate, but he was in their home. You really can't blame the bears."

He and his father flew to Montana, where John's remains were cremated, and drove the dead man's car back to Wisconsin.

It was, as Mark recalls, a long drive.

. . .

Back in Glacier, Charlie Logan was getting ready to pull some long shifts himself.

As the bad news circulated around the park that Sunday morning, Logan, Frain, and Wilde rose in the ranger cabin to find the weather had gone to hell. Plans had called for a helicopter to arrive at first light and carry the body to park headquarters, but fog had cut the visibility to about one hundred feet when the sun rose at a little after seven. By half past eight the temperature had fallen ten degrees, the wind had picked up, and snow was coming down in big round flakes. It wasn't until half past eleven that the weather cleared enough to bring a helicopter into the alpine bowl. On the way in, rangers spotted the bears on Petranyi's body. The sow had a distinctive marking—a light-colored collar of fur around her neck and descending onto her chest.

More armed rangers came in on that flight, and Buck Wilde rode the helicopter back to park headquarters. His role was over, but the rangers' work had hardly started.

It took a couple of hours to get the six rangers and helicopter pilot Jim Kruger organized and a strategy worked out. Five rangers would walk to Petranyi's body. One would fly in the helicopter with Kruger, to observe the operation from the air. The ground crew arrived at the site at 2:15 and found Petranyi's body had been moved another seventy-five feet, where the bears had eaten more of it.

Pilot Kruger found the bear family—a sow and two cubs—still near the body. The bears didn't want to leave and kept trying to get closer, so he started hazing them with the helicopter, trying to keep them away from the body and the ground crew. "He'd get her going one way, and then she would come back another way," Logan says. All this information was traveling to the ground crew via radio, but it was still hard to pinpoint the bears' exact location. It took only twenty minutes to load the body in the airship—four men carrying and one standing guard, keeping a close eye on the bushes—but it was a long twenty minutes. Then the ground crew continued documenting all the evidence they could find, working under a constant guard. With the helicopter gone, nobody knew where the bears were. As they backtracked to the site of the backpack and camera and fanned out to search some more, the crew found Petranyi's wallet in the woods, a dozen steps from his backpack.

The wallet allowed the rangers to positively identify him and also provided a crucial piece of evidence. It had been torn by bear teeth, gouged deep enough to puncture the plastic credit cards inside it. There were a few traces of blood on the wallet and a little more blood on a nearby tree. That was enough to indicate that Petranyi had initially been attacked there and had then moved closer to the trail, where

Wilde had found the pool of blood. Probably he had rested there, bleeding, and then moved down the trail the way he had come, hoping to find help.

Buck Wilde believes Petranyi met the bears in a surprise encounter, that the bears were running from the cooking area of the campground (tracks showed one bear had come within fifteen yards of Wilde while he ate breakfast), and that, when they ran into Petranyi, the mother attacked to defend her cubs.

Rangers, who had more time to investigate, came up with a handful of possible scenarios. Since the pack and camera appeared to have been laid carefully down, and because Petranyi's pants and underwear were around his ankles when he was found, they said it was possible that he had placed his things beside the trail and moved into the woods for a bowel movement or to urinate. That's where the bear hit him first. Then either she let him go or he escaped and moved back to the trail, where he stopped long enough to leave the pool of blood before moving downhill, back toward his car and the only source of help he knew about.

It's also possible that he saw the bears on the trail and set his gear down before running into the woods, where the bears caught up with him. Under this scenario they may have charged before or after he started running.

Maybe he saw the bears and put his things down, preparing to photograph them, and they attacked.

Or he could have heard a noise and moved into the woods, leaving his gear behind, to investigate.

The bowel movement theory seems likely but is not conclusive. The only evidence backing it up is that his pants were down around his ankles. But being dragged by a bear shredded his shirt and pulled a boot off his foot. It could easily have pulled his pants down, too. Besides, if he had stepped into the woods to relieve himself, why would he leave his hat in the trail? Unless, of course, he dropped the hat after being attacked, as he stumbled back to the trail. Rangers found his glasses and some other items in the woods, indicating considerable movement in a small area.

It's clear that the initial assault didn't kill him.

The blood spots that Wilde followed down the Loop Trail were round, indicating Petranyi probably walked down the trail under his own power. If the bear had dragged him down the trail, the blood would have been smeared. Also, the bear left claw marks on the trail but no pad marks, indicating the bear was up on its toes, running.

Less than six hundred feet from the pack and camera, the bear caught Petranyi again, causing the "thrashing" marks in the trail. That's probably where he died. Then it dragged him down the trail a few steps and into the woods, where Wilde would find him.

It's possible that the bear chased Petranyi down the trail, but "he probably bumped into the bear again there," Logan says.

It is those last six hundred feet of his brother's travels that bother Mark Petranyi the most.

"Apparently, he attempted to get away," Mark says. "Maybe that was the wrong thing to do. We'll never know. But that time from the first attack until she finally got him . . . it must have been sheer terror. Why didn't the bear go away? I've asked myself that question a thousand times."

Rangers asked themselves the same question. A grizzly bear had killed and eaten a man. It was an incredibly rare situation. In the ninety-year history of Glacier Park, where thousands upon thousands of people walk through grizzly country every year, Petranyi was only the ninth person to be killed by a grizzly bear. And in most of those cases, the bear left the body alone after the attack. During the same period, forty-eight people drowned in the park, twenty-three fell to their deaths from cliffs, and twenty-six died in car wrecks. Clearly, grizzly bears are only one of many perils in the park.

"In all my other cases, the bear attacks, neutralizes the threat, and leaves," Logan says.

The National Park Service met Monday morning to discuss the situation. Logan and the other rangers flew to park headquarters to participate. Chief Ranger Steve Frye called some outside bear experts for advice. After a few hours, the group of rangers and administrators decided the bears must die.

A combination of circumstances led to that decision. The initial attack on Petranyi may have been a defensive reaction by a surprised bear, and that is not normally a death sentence for a bear in Glacier National Park. But it quickly turned into a "predatory" situation when she started eating him. Add the bear's aggression on the trail, the way she had tried to buck the helicopter to get back to the corpse, and the way she had partially buried the body. Then add public and political perceptions.

"By removing that bear we perhaps saved many bears," Logan says.

That sounds like stilted logic at first, but it makes sense in the highly charged political debates over grizzly bears and their place in the modern world. If the bear had been allowed to live, "then," says Logan, "every attack after that would have been the man-killing grizzly" in the public mind.

"We're trying to have an atmosphere where people and bears can coexist," he says. But having a bear around that has earned a food reward by killing a person "is not consistent with what we want to achieve here. It was terrible to have to remove that grizzly bear, but I never had any second thoughts about it."

Logan and several other rangers packed up their weapons and flew back to the chalet at Granite Park.

· · ·

The rangers searched from the air for as long as the weather held out that day but couldn't find the bears they were looking for. A family group was spotted a few miles away, but they were the wrong bears.

That night snow fell, and by the next morning—day four of the incident—a couple of inches of fresh dust coated the high country.

Kruger flew in part of a rancid deer carcass to use as bait, carrying it in a sling beneath his helicopter. Rangers on the ground had to adjust the bait, manipulating the smelly carcass and knowing there were hungry grizzlies in the area. Later that afternoon a large, chocolate-colored grizzly came in, sniffed the bait, and disappeared with the whole bundle in less than five seconds as rangers watched through binoculars. Bait would be staked to the ground in the future.

The hunt was marked with frustration. Several snares were set and baited with more deer carcasses, but they didn't do the job. The rangers caught a grizzly one day, but he was the wrong animal, a subadult male, so they let him go. Bear biologists with the Montana Department of Fish, Wildlife and Parks flew in to help. Bear sign was everywhere. Rangers on foot patrol found tracks of the bear family in one of the places where Petranyi's body had lain, along the trail where he had been dragged, and in nearby meadows. They found places where bears had "rototilled" their previous day's footsteps as they dug up roots. Rangers spotted the bears a couple of times over the next several days, but nobody could get a shot at them.

It wasn't until October 11, day nine of the incident, that they were finally killed. Kruger had spotted them while shuttling rangers in and out of the chalet area. But there was a problem. Another family of bears was in the same area. The rangers had to make sure they were shooting the right bears, so Logan and Ranger Regi Altop climbed into the helicopter and buzzed over the bears several times until Logan saw what he was looking for: that light-colored collar around the sow's neck.

Kruger dropped the two rangers off about two hundred yards from the bears, and they crept closer while the helicopter hovered overhead. The bears paid little attention to the noisy chopper and focused on digging up roots, a testament to the single-minded quest for food that grizzlies display in the fall.

When the rangers approached within one hundred yards, they took careful aim at the feeding sow with their .300 H&H Magnum rifles. Logan started counting. When he hit three, both men fired. The sow took a couple of steps and fell dead. Then they opened fire on the cubs. One dropped, and the other took off into the woods, wounded but still scampering.

More rangers arrived to help Logan and Altop search for the wounded animal, and after about an hour, Kruger spotted it from the helicopter. The four rangers spread out and went after it, walking uphill.

That's when the second bear family showed up.

Kruger had to take his eyes off the cub and haze the second family away with his helicopter, trying to keep them away from the rangers, trying to keep a bad situation from getting worse fast. It worked, but the men lost the cub.

Kruger, always sharp-eyed, spotted the cub later in the day with a spotting scope that was set up at the chalet. It had come back to the area where its mother had died, wounded and alone. Kruger flew Steve Frye and another ranger to the area. It was almost dark by then, but they walked into a thick stand of trees and finished the animal off with a final shot.

At 6:43 p.m. on the eleventh day of October 1992, after nine bloody and grueling days, Kruger loaded the cub into his helicopter and lifted off for the last time. The whole unpleasant business was finally over.

■ ■ ■

The three bear carcasses were shipped to the Montana Department of Fish, Wildlife and Parks diagnostic laboratory in Bozeman, Montana, where veteran biologist Keith Aune performed a necropsy, an autopsy for animals.

The National Park Service wanted to know if there was any evidence of Petranyi inside the bears, any hair or flesh or fiber. Bear scat collected near Petranyi's body contained human remains and two different types of cloth. But when Aune examined the bears, he found nothing unusual. Not that he had expected much. The bears had been passing huge amounts of food through their bodies in the days since Petranyi died. Each of them had a belly full of roots when it died.

Rangers singled these bears out for death working on the best possible evidence. They had seen these bears near the body and trying to get closer. There was no other family group in the area with cubs that size. But had they killed Petranyi? The rangers were sure, but they wanted scientific evidence, something to remove absolutely all doubt about whether they had killed the right bears. Aune couldn't give it to them. Sophisticated DNA tests, common now, weren't readily available at the time.

"There was no evidence in the stomach or gastrointestinal tract which can confirm the presence" of the bears at the scene of Petranyi's death.

A niggling doubt would remain forever, and that's the kind of thing that can bother a park ranger. People don't sign up to be rangers because they enjoy killing grizzly bears.

"It's beyond a reasonable doubt," says Glacier spokeswoman Amy Vanderbilt, whose husband, Ranger Gary Moses, helped investigate the incident. "But we'll never be able to absolutely verify it."

Aune did, however, provide some information about the bears. The sow was at least fifteen years old, in good general health, and weighed 251 pounds. She harbored a normal load of parasites, was seventy-four inches long, and carried a layer of fat an inch thick along her back, indicating she was only in moderate shape. Bears often have two to four inches of fat along their backs at that time of year. Her two cubs, both females, weighed thirty-nine pounds and fifty pounds.

The sow's left front foot had been injured recently, which could have caused an attitude problem, but the most interesting thing Aune found was in her mouth: deep cavities in her molars.

"They had to be very painful," Aune says. Also, one of her front teeth had rotted away almost entirely.

Did a constant and severe toothache make the bear more cantankerous? Aune, who has studied grizzlies for decades, thinks it probably did.

But why did she run away from Buck Wilde as he ate breakfast, then attack Petranyi twice and feed on him? Seeing Wilde was probably no surprise to her. She knew the area, knew that people were often seen in the campground and cooking area. Whether she first saw Petranyi on the trail or in the woods, it likely was a surprise encounter, which triggered an instinct to protect her cubs. The toothache probably reduced her tolerance level at least a little. That, combined with her intense focus on calories prior to denning for the winter, could have triggered some kind of switch that made her see Petranyi as food rather than as a nuisance or a threat and made her attack a second time and begin to eat him.

. . .

Buck Wilde says it took him five years before he could talk about the incident with any comfort.

When the helicopter took him to park headquarters, rangers interviewed him again, then repeated Logan's earlier advice to get some psychological counseling—"to make sure from a shrink point of view that everything was sort of okay," is the way Wilde puts it.

He declined. Rather, he shouldered his backpack and slipped out the back door of the headquarters building, dodging the reporters waiting for him at the front door. Then he walked to the highway, stuck out his thumb, and caught a ride with a couple he had met two days earlier while hiking in to Granite Park. He told them the story, and the man bought him a bottle of Wild Turkey whiskey ("It's one of my poisons, especially in high-stress situations") before dropping him at a trailhead on the east side of the park.

Wilde was seeking his own mental therapy.

"I decided I was going back into bear country."

It was an area new to him, the Triple Divide Pass, where waters run to the Atlantic, the Pacific, and Hudson Bay.

"I wasn't just scared, I was scared to death. I had been shaken, fundamentally, to the core. I wanted to handle my shakiness in a way that would be constructive, and I thought the most constructive thing to do, for my psyche, was to get back in bear country. Fear management, I guess you'd call it."

He's had other big scares since then. A couple of more charges by grizzlies and a canoe wreck that left him stranded on an island in the raging North Fork of the Flathead River for six days.

He doesn't like to talk about that one much either, for the same reason he's avoided talking much about the Petranyi incident.

"It's taken me five years to get to the point where I'm ready to do that. You get kind of weird when you spend as much time in the woods as I do. I understand firsthand what is meant by the word 'taboo.' Taboos are things that the Native Americans dealt with in special terms, by whispering or whatever."

He's still a little uncomfortable talking about it. It brings things back, he says, and he wants to treat the situation with respect for the bears and for Petranyi's family. And there is another matter. Call it practical spirituality. Long-term physical survival in the wilderness depends on having the right attitude, Wilde believes.

"I felt that if I didn't give this situation enough respect, spiritually, and with all the time I spend in bear country, the bears would get me. That sounds pretty weird, but it's really the way I look at it. One thing you should get is that I was scared shitless. It scared me enough to make it very special."

He says he doesn't expect people to understand him, but he believes what he believes. It's important to him.

The trip into Triple Divide Pass lasted five days. He saw lots of bear sign, tracks, and evidence of fresh digging. But he didn't see a bear during the whole trip, and today he's comfortable in the woods.

Put yourself in Buck Wilde's shoes.

What would you have done?

POSTSCRIPT

Buck Wilde still spends a lot of time with grizzly bears. Every summer he guides tourists into the isolated coastal zone in Alaska, where controversial bear advocate Timothy Treadwell was famously mauled to death and eaten in 2003. He's good enough at this work that some people now call him a "bear whisperer." When he's not in Alaska, he's publishing books of his photography and giving what he calls "enrichment presentations." He now has twenty years of experience living with grizzlies and often finds himself within a few yards of them.

He says he makes it a point not to push his luck. Unlike Treadwell he knows the bears aren't going to fall in love with him. But if he's careful, they put up with him.

"There are some real fundamentals, and if you follow them, bears are real tolerant," he says. "You can become comfortable working with them, as a photographer."

Never approach a bear, he says. Don't try sneaking or zigzagging around. It won't work. Rather, let the bear see you, and let it approach you on its own terms and move at its own speed. Sitting down is the least threatening posture, he says.

"Just plant yourself, and be willing to pay the price that photographers pay," he says. "The bears will come check you out. Are you a threat? Are you benign?"

"Don't try to be cute," he says. "You can trip that wire, and there will be a result." If you disturb the bear, chances are it will run away. But it might charge.

If a bear does charge, stand your ground. Don't hit the ground and curl up unless a bear knocks you down. Never, never run. "That's the golden, golden rule," Wilde says.

None of his clients have been injured, and many have come home with remarkable images and footage.

Cases like Petranyi's are incredibly rare. Wilde stresses that.

"He was a victim of circumstance," Wilde said. "But I feel like I'm on a mission to show the other side of the bear. I've designed a kinship with the bear. But it will take a better psychiatrist than me to decipher it."

LAND OF TREMBLING EARTH
CHARLES ELLIOTT

A simple fishing and photography trip into one of the most interesting wilderness areas on the planet turns into a survival experience in this compelling tale by Outdoor Life *magazine's veteran Southeastern region field editor, the late Charles Elliott. Because I had the privilege of knowing Charlie so well during my stint as editor of* Outdoor Life, *I can vouch for every word of his prose being both true and accurate. Here his engaging storytelling ability puts you in his boot steps as he faces the daunting task of making his way out of Georgia's great Okefenokee Swamp without a boat. The journey is a reading experience you will not soon forget.*

. . .

I had to have some pictures of a blackfish. In case you've never heard of a blackfish, let me introduce you to him. He has other names—quite a variety of them, as bowfin, grindle, mudfish, scaled ling, lawyer ling and a dozen other appellations he has acquired in the past thirty or forty million years since he passed blithely through the epochs and ages when other vertebrates appeared, prospered and disappeared from the face of the earth. I've met him a good many times in the sluggish waters of the southern states and each time I am tremendously impressed by my contact. He is the only fish I know that just doesn't give a damn for falling barometers, solunar theories and tables, distant oceanic tides or the weather.

Any time in sluggish waters within his range that you fish for him with the proper tackle and the proper bait in his darkened home, you are likely to find yourself tied into a long, dark fish with all the tricks of a rodeo pony and the power of a snorkel sub.

One of the remarkable abilities of the black fish is his knack of surviving for long periods out of water. Except for some of the lung fishes which curl up in the mud when the water goes out of their home and live on soggy air until the lake is replenished, the blackfish holds a caudal to no finned creature, not even the versatile mudcat. Like the gar, the blackfish has a lung, built with a network of blood vessels and can breathe out of the water as well as in it.

The best place I knew to get the kind of pictures I wanted was on the rim of the Okefenokee Swamp, with the help of my old friend, Lem Griffis.

J. L. Stephens, who has sat with me around many a campfire, went along to help me get my photographs. With Lem we paddled up one of the narrow creeks that wound along the rim of the swamp. The bass were striking, but we had to catch a blackfish.

"Now that you've tried all your plugs and spinners," Lem said, "get your camera ready. I'll make 'em jump for you."

Before he left home, he had cut half a dozen fresh pieces of pork from just under a bacon rind. Weighting his line with a sinker, he hooked on one of the two inch pieces of meat. Throwing this into a deep, black hole, he worked it slowly across the bottom of the river. His short rod suddenly arched in his hands.

"Git ready!" Lem yelled. "Here he comes!"

He set back on the rod tip and the black fish took to the

air, in a series of acrobatics which so astounded me that I forgot to snap the shutter of my camera. But it didn't make too much difference that I missed the first picture. Lem knew how to make those fish hit a pork rind when they wouldn't take an artificial lure. All morning he brought them spinning into the air, crashing the surface of the river. One even jumped completely over a low-hanging limb above the water, breaking his line so that Lem had to rig up again.

Although he is generally classed as an undesirable individual in the fishing waters from Canada to Florida, I certainly would have cast my vote for him that afternoon. Those fish Lem hooked were savage strikers and bulldog battlers.

The blackfish doesn't jump as furiously or as many times as the normal black bass that weighs around three or four pounds. After hitting the surface of the water in a violent effort to throw the bait, he settles down to a tenacious fight against the backbone of the rod, shaking his head with the obstinate determination of a bull. And when he comes to the boat, he comes in like a hooked alligator, twisting over and over in the water, trying to tear the barbed steel from his jaws.

And we got the pictures—a wonderful set of photographs with fish in the air, twisting, turning, and in a couple of instances just as the air-bourne grindle threw our hook back at the boat.

When I had put my camera up for the day, we made a long run up one of the black water trails that led back into the depths of this drowned hinterland I had known intimately for years. It was like seeing an old friend again.

Volumes have been written about the great swamp, but it's the men who have shared its sunshine and rain, its brooding loneliness, pristine beauty, and its eternal threat of disaster; who really know its secrets. A geologist once told me that the Okefenokee sits on top of a hill. He proved his contention by pointing out that the St. Marys River flows out of the eastern side and creeps a hundred miles to the Atlantic Ocean, while the Suwanee pours over its southern rim and races down its twisted channel some six hundred miles to the Gulf of Mexico.

The altitude of the swamp is a hundred and thirty feet above sea level, and it perches between thirty to forty feet above the surrounding country. It is in the shape of a huge mud cup and was formed by the action of Archaic seas. The geologists think that the Okefenokee was originally a lake, but in the past eras has developed into a morass, approximately a thousand square miles in size, including its wilderness borders.

Okefenokee is an Indian word which means "trembling earth." It gets its name from the prairies, those expansive open areas of marsh made up from floating islands of peat, on which grass and other seeds have sprouted. Over the years these islands have grown together into a mass of floating land, broken only by a few runs and trails through them.

The floating bog will support the weight of a man if he moves continuously across it. A heavy, motionless object will quickly break through the artificial, rubbery earth and plunge out of sight into the black water beneath. By stamping his feet, a man can set the land for many yards around him to quivering like a field of jelly, and I have seen Lem Griffis push a twenty foot pole out of sight into the muck.

Abundant wildlife moves on land, and in the air and water of the swamp. It was one of the last homes of such species as the southern panther and ivory-billed woodpecker.

The character of this wild hilltop garden has changed but little in the past centuries, in spite of the ravages of man. A quarter of a century ago or more, railroads were built on pilings into many parts of the Okefenokee and the virgin cypress lumber, millions upon millions of feet, were brought out over the stilted road bed.

Eventually the trains steamed out to more orthodox road beds, most of the pilings rotted down and the reaching fingers of nature's vines and trees and other vegetation, covered the scars. The logging camps, once roaring with rough activity, have fallen into decay and settled to become once more a part of the earth's restless mold. Nature has kindly blotted out the desecration and healed the wounds made by man's avidness.

There is something timeless and eternal about the Okefenokee Swamp. You feel it when you stand under the slim bodied pines on Billy's Island, or pause in the big cypress grove on Minnie Lake to taste the ceaseless but unhurried tenor of life that moves about you.

Among the rare features of the swamp is its water. Vegetable dyes have stained it the color of ebony, but back off the beaten trails, it is as sweet and pure as a mountain brook. Islands, peopled with pines and oaks and laced with palmettoes, are scattered bits of topography. The lakes are elongated, winding mirrors, trimmed in gray and emerald, kaleidoscopic with bright plumaged birds.

The average visitor may travel hundreds of miles within the morass and see only a small part of it. Except for the canal on the Folkston side, the only byways are narrow, black-water trails connecting the lakes and landings of the islands and mainland.

In the past there has been tremendous outside pressure to open trails to all portions of the swamp. Instead, the existing trails have been allowed to grow up with the result that this vegetative dam holds back the flow and maintains a stable water level.

If it were not for the guides and alligators, the prairies would eventually close up altogether. The deep holes are the homes of gators, which keep them clear of the marching lilies and grasses.

Lem and his guides, usually in a hurry, tear through the swamp from one lake to another, grinding the aquatic verdure out of the way. The precision and skill with which Lem handles a motor is amazing to anyone without webs between his toes. He misses stumps by the breadth of a hair, tears through bonnet patches—the bonnet is a type of lily found in the swamp—and jumps sunken logs, sometimes throwing his boat almost completely out of the water.

Personally I prefer that Lem leave his motor at home. A paddled boat does not provide the physical thrills, but it makes possible a deeper and more lasting impression of the Okefenokee. Without the noise, the sinuous trails become an adventure in solitude, in flights of birds that drift through the trees, in acre after acre of wild orchids, in eight and ten foot alligators which appear suddenly under the boat and then vanish again into the depths.

Colossal-minded citizens have proposed to cut a canal between the Atlantic Ocean and Gulf of Mexico through the Okefenokee. This proposal, along with other schemes to drain the swamp for agricultural purposes, build scenic highways through it and otherwise develop it commercially, died with the purchase of some half million acres of lake area in the heart of the sodden space by the federal government, for use as a migratory waterfowl refuge.

When the refuge went under federal protection in 1935, wildlife in the region was at an all time low. The huge ivory-billed woodpecker had either been killed out or moved on in front of the logging trails. Ornithologists claim there is a possibility that the ivorybills still reside in the big gum slough at the south end of the swamp. Alligators had been slaughtered in tremendous numbers for their hides. This destruction was evident in piles of saurian bones scattered throughout the area. One heap of skeletons I saw on Billy's Island was higher than a man's head. A glimpse of an alligator, except in remote corners of the Okefenokee, was a rare occurrence.

None of the birds were spared by native gunners. The whooping crane, once so plentiful, disappeared. Even the Florida cranes, brother to the sandhill crane which darkened primitive Midwestern skies, were reduced to stragglers. The otters, minks and raccoons kept the fur houses of the nearby towns generously supplied with prime pelts.

On a two weeks camping trip into the swamp in 1933, I found three brothers living in the drowned forest, east of Bigwater Lake. They had constructed a pole platform above the water level, erected a thatch palmetto roof over it and piled in heaps of Spanish moss for bedding. They existed chiefly on the wildlife, eating mudfish, terrapins, woodpeckers, and any creature they could kill or capture near their camp. They went outside only a few times each year to trade their hides and furs for gunshells, salt, corn squeezings and the other bare necessities of life.

These three hundred and sixty five day a year hunters living in and around the Okefenokee, had killed the breeding stock of most large species down to such a low ebb that to bring them back, absolute protection was essential. But years of constant vigilance and protection have paid dividends in the increase of all forms of swamp life. On spring nights the earth resounds with the roars of big bull alligators. In the crotch of almost any tall cypress, the masked face of a raccoon may be seen peering intently down upon oblivious fishermen. Since the no-trapping regulation was put into effect, the raccoons have increased a third of a million, by the latest estimate. Otter trails criss-cross with the man made runs. Bears are more plentiful than they have been in the memory of the old timers around the refuge.

The too abundant bruin population has become a headache to the officials who administer the area, especially those bears living within the protection of the swamp and forage outside on bee colonies and hogs of the natives.

Recently a trapping program was inaugurated to move a part of the bear tribe to other portions of the south. This was done only after one local citizen set out to destroy all the fur-coated blacks. He was making good progress when two federal game wardens discovered him inside the refuge with a gun. He ran and they sprinted after him. Finding himself trapped by a maze of sloughs, he swung quickly and threw up his double barrel, loaded with buckshot. In cold blood he killed both wardens, left them in the edge of the swamp where they fell.

When the bodies of the two men were found, sharp-eyed FBI agents noted that the only natives absent from the scene of the crime were the hunter and his family. They went to question him.

"Yep," he said, without hesitation. "I done it. They were protectin' th' b'ars that et up all my pigs an' honey. I'd do it ag'in."

He readily returned with them and helped to reconstruct the chain of incidents leading up to the murder.

"Th' bears," Lem agreed, "are gettin' as thick as they were that time I helped th' tourister ketch a cub."

To Lem all strangers are touristers. They are his main source of bread and butter. It seems that this particular tourister got such a severe scratching that he was "durn glad of it" when the little bear got away.

One of the amazing facts about the Okefenokee is that fishing has been excellent throughout all its periods of desecration. While other wildlife species disappeared, bream, bass, perch and pickerel held their own. Some twenty thousand fishermen and sightseers a year come from all over the nation to try their luck in the dark waters and to take away countless strings of fish.

It would seem that since otters, alligators and sharp beaked birds had increased in such tremendous numbers, they might be eating more fish than the waters could grow. I have been assured by the experts that these fishing predators help rather than hurt the fishing, since they consume the slower, undesirable species, leaving more water space for the game fish. Then too, the vast, inaccessible portions of the swamp are a reservoir for those areas the average fisherman is unable to reach.

One of the most interesting experiences I ever had in the Okefenokee Swamp was almost my last. In a little home-made canoe, with our duffle piled between us in the middle of the boat, Steve and I plowed up Billy Lake for more than a mile, then turned north into a narrow black water trail that wound into the cypress forest.

A brief storm the hour before had left the air cool and no air currents reached down into the cypress trees. The ebon water was a mirror that gave back reflections of the drowned forest in lovely color tones. Once we started a half grown alligator from his log beside the water trail. He splashed into the lake, shattering the mirror, then his eyes and long snout appeared on the surface and he glided out of sight into a bonnet patch.

After almost three hours of steady paddling up the crooked run, the water trail broadened and deepened into a channel that curved into the trees.

"We'll camp here for the night," Steve suggested, "and get into that country around Hickory Hammock tomorrow."

I remembered that pole platform, built about four feet above the water. One of the guides had constructed it there, as a resting place for his fishing parties, many miles from solid earth.

We pulled our tiny craft beside the platform and unloaded our supplies. While Steve collected wood for a fire from the dead branches of the standing trees, I clicked my rod together and paddled up the lake. The bass were striking just at dusk and I brought in two largemouths which had mistaken my wooden frog for the real McCoy. I cleaned the fish and handed them to my woodsman friend, who had built his campfire on a wide, heavy piece of tin the guides kept in the shelter for that purpose.

While Steve completed the meal, I arranged the beds on a base of Spanish moss and put up the mosquito netting. The vicious little insects had already collected around the camp-fire light and lost no time in sitting down to dine on tender city meat.

Our fish were fresh and sweet as new butter, but we didn't have time to give them the culinary courtesy they were due. I threw mine down like a famished wolf and beat off the swarming horde before I crawled into the bunk.

"I don't like this wild goose chase," Steve said from his sleeping bag. "Let's come back in here later when the bugs are not quite as hungry or ill tempered."

I listened for a moment to the night sounds all around us. Not a note was out of tune. From somewhere beyond the lake a barrel owl laughed with his crazy hunting cry and just beyond our very doorstep an alligator boomed his bellowing roar. The drowsy chorus of tree frogs lapsed into startled silence, then one by one took up the chant again.

"They're not too bad in the daylight," I murmured, "and I want to find that lake with lunker bass."

"I know the way in, all right," Steve replied, "but we don't know how rough the going will be. The canoe you insisted we bring along is built like a paper napkin, and any cypress knee may punch a hole clean through it."

With the darkness pressing down close all around us, I was too relaxed even to reply.

The smell of wood smoke in my face awoke me. The sun was surging upward beyond the lake and shafts of rose colored light stabbed through the cypress grove. A few of the mosquitoes still clung close around our camp, but the heavy flight of insects had gone back into the forest in search of less illusive prey. I washed my face at the edge of the platform and packed our equipment while Steve finished cooking breakfast. The sun slid on into the flat-topped cypress and the long, dark shadows changed to grayish gold.

We paddled through the veil of mist clinging on the water, and worked our way out of the upper end of the lake through a twisted trail. Where the heavy forest came to an abrupt wall, the prairie began, and the swamp was open except for scattered clumps of cypress and myrtle trees.

To Steve this section of the swamp was like his own back yard. A hundred water trails sprawled out like tangled ribbons through the morass, and all but one had a blind ending in some far reach of the spongy earth. Steve selected the right path winging through the maze, and turned into an obscure runway which might have been left by a raccoon or otter through the lily pads.

We quickly left the deep black water of the main runs and plowed through the thickest sponge of earth I ever saw. There was not enough water to float even the small canoe, so we crawled out on the floating land.

"If you break through," Steve warned, "hold on to the side of the boat. And keep your eyes peeled for moccasins. If a big, rusty cottonmouth ever hits you, there won't be any need to even try to get you back to the landing."

I slogged through the floating land in front of the boat, dragging at its bow. Steve trailed, pushing the stern of the craft, lifting it over rough spots where roots and stumps showed through the marsh. We were not out of sight of the run when I almost stepped on a moccasin. The grass clump where he was coiled, patterned his body perfectly. His head was in a position to strike, as though he dared me to take one more step. I had a funny feeling that it would be wise not to call his bluff.

"I'll show you what it means to be careful," Steve said.

He struck out a canoe paddle and the snake struck it so fast and savagely that we could not even see its head move. The blow half turned the paddle in Steve's hand, and the moccasin coiled with amazing speed. My partner pulled in the paddle blade and we examined it. A fang had broken off in the soft, wood, which was smeared with thick, yellow poison.

"There's enough venom there," Steve grunted, "to wipe out your family for three generations before you were born."

We crushed out the snake's life and moved on. From that moment I kept my eyes on the ground, watching for the coils of death. So intently did I examine the trembling earth directly in front of the canoe that Steve had to call the turns of the trail for me.

It was hot! My clothes were wringing wet with brine and narrow rivulets of salt water poured down my face and neck. The dim trail led into a huge alligator hole out in the prairie. We climbed back into the canoe for a brief rest. Steve loaded his pipe and passed the tobacco up to me.

"I don't like this," he said, frankly.

I was hot and tired and as wet as if I had been soused head first into the gator hole. My words were sharp.

"Then get out and walk back," I advised.

He didn't answer and I felt a funny sensation at the base of my scalp. I wanted to eat those words, because I knew he was right. We were already off the beaten path and on our own. No one knew we were there and no one would come looking for us.

The alligator cave was fifty feet or more across. There was no sign of the old saurian, which had probably gone to the bottom when he heard us approach through the marsh.

We took the trail which ran northwest out of the open water and were soon on our feet again, dragging the canoe. The craft was light as a feather and either of us could pick it up with one hand, but in the floating earth it held us back with the drag of a crippled scow, and by noon my legs were rubbery.

We stopped on the prairie and ate a piece of bread and slab of cheese the size of my hand. That was our lunch. The water here was shallow and tepid, so we rinsed our mouth out and smoked for half an hour before we plowed on through the trembling earth.

I began to realize that this trip back into the interior of the Okefenokee, bass or no bass, was not all I had anticipated. I began to wonder, too, if we would make the edge of the timber by dark, since it was necessary to walk with such extreme care and with so great an effort. A night in the trees would be miserable enough, but a night out on the prairie, where we had no protection, would be infinitely worse. The snakes hunted at night, as well as during the day, and we wouldn't dare move around and chance stepping on a venom-loaded spiral.

Although I was pooped almost to the point of paralysis, I turned on fresh steam to reach the rim of the timber before dark. Steve pulled on the stern and stopped the canoe.

"Take it easy," he cautioned, "or we'll never make it."

Slowly, almost imperceptibly, the fringe of woods crept closer. The sun inched down its trail into the western sky and the air grew very still. We stopped to rest out on the bog and in the swelling silence, I suddenly heard the drums. The drums are sounds which are sometimes heard in the vast and empty spaces of the earth. Science has never been able to explain them in a satisfactory manner. They may be caused by an infinitesimal movement of a geological fault line. They may be due in the swamp to the bursting of gas bubbles, or they may be caused by something that defies natural explanation. The only place I ever heard them was in the Okefenokee Swamp. Like some ancient ceremonial rite of Indian tribes, they intoned a steady rhythm that beat against my ears and eyes and soaked into my skin. I could literally feel the pulsating throb. The drums of silence, of vast empty spaces, the chant of far-flung hinterlands—the ceremony of the gods!

I could not stop the quiver that ran the length of my sun-parched frame. I didn't look around, but I could feel that Steve was as tense as stretched gut. Those were ominous sounds that every swamper dreaded as an omen of bad luck. I set my teeth against them and laughed.

"What the hell?" I said. "You've heard the drums before."

My canoe mate did not laugh, or even reply.

Twilight was gathering around the edge of the timber and was beginning to melt down over the swamp, when we pulled into the cypress. I was as limp as a dirty sponge. A stretch of open water bordered the trees. I swung the front end of the canoe into this semi lake which sliced through the wooded rim and opened into a huge alligator hole. Steve pointed out a tall heap of grass and sticks rearing its dome at the end of the lake.

"Young 'gators," he whispered.

On the mound I could see a dozen of the tiny reptiles, which resembled overgrown fence lizards. Then we detected the old gator herself, moving across the upper end of her black home. Instead of submerging and sinking her armour plated body into the mud, she swung around and plowed in the direction of our boat, snorting and blowing a mist of water out of her nostrils.

"Pull ashore," Steve yelled.

Something in his tone kept me from laughing. Alligators are creatures of fierce appearance, but normally they are not dangerous. Only under the most extraordinary circumstances will they tackle a man. One of those circumstances could be that they have never seen a man. Somehow Steve knew that this old gal meant business.

I dug my paddle in and swung the bow of the canoe toward the edge of the timber. I felt Steve's powerful stroke. The light craft shuddered under his corded arms and leapt forward. For a moment in the excitement I lost my sense of caution. The thin canoe suddenly splintered under my feet and I was half thrown out into the dark water. I managed to maintain my balance, but it was impossible to act quickly enough to save the craft. The end of the jagged stump sliced through the thin layer of paint, canvas and narrow lathe as though it had been parched newsprint.

I wrenched the boat away from the stump—too late. The canoe was flooded and sinking beneath us.

"Look out!"

I jumped for shore. The alligator, unfrightened even by this flurry of excitement, was almost upon us. I released my paddle and pulled myself up into the cypress roots fringing the hole. Steve was knee deep in the thick edge, with water running out of his hat, shirt and pants.

"I knew we were in for trouble," he said, "as soon as I got a look at those baby gators on the grass heap."

Two pieces of our canoe floated on the surface. I thought bitterly that the only combination of reasons an alligator out in the wild would charge any creature larger than herself was to protect her young and because she had never seen a man, and we had been on the receiving end of both. I felt a stab of pain in my neck. It came from a mosquito. Suddenly, with the excitement of the skirmish over, I realized our predicament. We were more than ten miles from land in any direction. Not ordinary miles, but in the middle of a venom infested swamp. Our supplies and equipment had gone down with the canoe into an alligator cave guarded by a zealous mother. On all sides of us lay the Okefenokee, where the life of a man afoot was not worth a handful of sulphur in Hades.

Out of the corner of my eye I saw that Steve was watching me with a bleak, expressionless squint. The blame was mine. No need to deny that, even to myself. I had insisted on coming to find this hidden lake and on bringing the light canoe. I remembered that Lem had shrugged his shoulders as if he never again expected to see us alive. He knew that a boat-less man didn't have a fifty-fifty chance of survival in this hot, reptile infested swamp. When they searched for us a week and then gave up the trail, the old swamper would wag his shock of hair.

"I tole 'em not t' take to th' swamp in that there cloth boat," he'd say.

The thought gave me a sudden jolt. With tremendous effort I shook off the quiver of alarm, and tried to convince myself that we had experienced a normal accident in a slightly more than normal way and we'd wade out. But I knew it wouldn't be normal wading, like a trout stream or in the backwash of the surf.

Steve hadn't said a word. He turned and splashed away from the open water, heading back into the swamp.

"Where you going?" I asked, rather foolishly.

"You can stand there and wait for those canned groceries to float to the top," he replied without looking back. "I'm going to find a hummock where I can spend the night."

I followed him into the cypress grove. Hummocks were mounds of vegetation, common to the shallow water of the cypress thickets, and for all practical purposes, dry. We might even sleep a little if we could find one of the mounds not inhabited by snakes, and if the gallinippers did not carry us off, piece by piece.

The dusky spaces under the cypress trees were growing darker by the moment. I fought a growing panic. The sudden change of temperature from the sun out on the prairie to twilight under the trees, and from parched skin to sopping clothes, was uncomfortable. Twice in the gathering dusk, I stumbled and fell into cypress roots that jabbed against my belly like the blow of an alligator's tail.

The character of the cypress forest changed. Where it had been open, the vegetation grew so thick that we could hardly push our way through it. The water under the trees was from knee deep to our arm pits and the bottom was a tangle of poles, logs, cypress knees and sharp sticks—all so slippery that to even stand on our feet was an acrobatic miracle.

We ran into a solid wall of vegetation. In the semi darkness there seemed no possible way to go around or through it. Steve stopped and I splashed up to him, waist deep in the water and oozing mud.

"We're stuck," he said. "There's no chance of finding one of those hummocks when it's this dark. If we did, there'd probably be a dozen snakes on it. We'll have to spend the night here."

"Here?" I bellowed. "Up to our arses in water?"

"We got this far on a series of your ideas," he grated, "have you got any more?"

I clamped my ivories together. The mosquitoes had already found us. They were collecting on my back, face, forehead and hands. I had heard of men going off the beam from the white hot stings of the tiny insects.

"Water is softer than a feather bed," I said.

The attempt at humor failed miserably. It even irritated me.

"We might be a little more comfortable than we are now," Steve suggested. "Did you lose your knife?"

I felt in my pocket. The knife. It was wrapped in a wad of dollar bills—money that would have purchased us a steak trimmed in mushrooms, and a soft, white-sheeted bed—I snapped off that picture and started trimming off the bushes about a foot above the water line, as Steve had directed. Out of the shaking leaves and limbs, great swarms of mosquitoes poured into the air, collecting around us in a thick smog. I swore aloud.

"Hold it!" Steve called, from somewhere out in the darkness, "We've got a lot of this to take."

I attacked the bushes with a renewed vigor I did not feel and cleared off a space about five feet square. Splashing in the swamp beside me, Steve floated two logs up to the cleared space. They were dry, dead stubs he had pushed over in the muck. We placed these on the stubble of the bushes. Their buoyancy and the stiff stems I had traded blisters for, held them above the surface.

Next we piled the slashings of the bushes I had cut, making a crude platform on the logs. Steve brought in a great armload of Spanish moss and piled it on the heap. He scrambled on the uneven heap and helped me up beside him. The log raft shifted uncertainly for a moment under our weight and then settled to a solid foundation in the brush stubble.

"I've had better beds," Steve commented, "and a few worse ones."

By now the light was gone. Darkness had settled down over the Okefenokee as completely as if the gods had put a black lid on the heavens. Through the roof of cypress tops we could see the stars flaming in an arc across the dome of heavens. Faint starlight penetrated into the jungle of swamp vegetation. The mosquitoes were singing a weird, whining chorus that spanned the limits of the musical scale. I buttoned my shirt collar under my chin and pulled my hands as far as possible up into my sleeves, and resigned myself to a night of torture, with the hope that at least a ragged part of us would be left at dawn.

The swamp sounds were not as peaceful as they had been the night before. The cries of the hunting owls in the distance were not mellow or soft, but wild, weird screams that shattered the night above the flow of noises on all sides of our nest. The chant of green tree frogs around us was a desolate sound. The water worked continuously with the sound of living bodies, and once a sharp crash off to the left brought Steve's head up at an alert angle.

"Probably a foraging bear," he said.

Sleep was impossible. We tried to cover ourselves with the moss, but the army of mosquitoes bored through to us, driving their dagger bills in to the hilt. The Bastille torture chambers were soft stuff.

The night could not have been longer if it had passed in a thousand years. When the first gray streaks of dawn crept through the cypress tops, I was in a drugged, exhausted stupor. I had ceased to mind the mosquitoes any more. Steve shook me and I sat up, half conscious of my surroundings, but I could see that his face was a solid welt. My face was even worse. The reflection looking back at me out of the dark mirror when I stooped over to splash cool water on my skin was like a piece of raw beef. My pains went from my hair roots to my toes.

Steve put his foot against my seat and pushed me off the platform into the water. The shock of cold drove some of the lethargy out of my system. I came up spluttering.

"We got to get out of here," he stated. "We can't take many nights like this one."

I pulled up my belt a couple of notches to take care of breakfast and we worked our way back through the swamp to the gator cave with the thought that we might salvage some of our food and equipment. By the time we reached the hole, the sun had climbed above the edge of the prairie, and the gator was sprawled in its warm rays near the very snag we'd hit.

"Just our luck," Steve said, grimly. "I reckon we'd better concentrate on getting out alive and hungry."

I agreed. I wondered why I'd ever had an interest in the lost bass lake we'd set out to find. But I did feel a little more refreshed. The exercise had set my blood to racing again, and I was in much better shape to give this challenge of life and death the proper attention it deserved.

"We're almost due north of the landing," Steve guessed, looking up at the sun. "As near as I can figure, we're about ten miles away as a mosquito would fly."

With the sun on our left, we cut into the cypress swamp. I was tired and standing on my feet was even more difficult than it had been the night before. The sharp sticks under the water jabbed at my legs, plowing up skin where they cut through the cloth of my clothes.

The sun poured into the cypress grove and brought with it great swarms of yellow flies, which were even worse than the mosquitoes. The saffron insects brought blood where they set their teeth. I cut a sprig of myrtle and ineffectively fought them off as I stumbled through the swamp. I was so engrossed in this running battle that I hardly noticed the deepening water. Steve, wading ahead, suddenly plunged out of sight before my eyes. I braced myself to dive for him and his head appeared again. I caught his arm and pulled him back to shallow water.

"We'll have to circle this deep slough, and hope to hell it doesn't extend all the way across the swamp," he announced.

The most difficult job I ever had was back-tracking through the muck and slippery logs. We were losing valuable time and distance, which might mean the difference in getting out alive. We turned east with the water under our arm pits and the fervent wish that we wouldn't meet another gator as belligerent as the last one.

I lost track of the minutes and hours. It seemed that I had always gone on and on, stumbling and floundering through an eternity of hellish snags and mud and water. A breeze blew hard against my face and I looked up. We had come to the rim of the prairie. The sun was almost directly overhead. It almost blinded me after the dark interior of the cypress wilderness.

"Walking'll be easier here," Steve commented, "and a hell of a lot more dangerous."

He found two slender cypress trees growing at the edge of the woods. We cut these down with the pocket knife and trimmed off the tops, converting them into poles about twenty feet in length.

"They'll serve two purposes," Steve explained. "If you break through the marsh out there, throw the pole flat against the ground and hold on. They will also help keep off any ornery moccasin or alligator we happen to meet."

Hacking at the cypress with my small knife completed the crop of blisters I had started the night before. And to my growing assortment of miseries, my body began to itch with the authority of the seven year kind. My skin was covered with welts, made by chigger bites. A whole colony of the microscopic red bugs had buried under my skin, probably from the moss bed, and set up housekeeping.

Walking across the floating morass was much more simple than wading up to our necks in the cypress grove, but we had to be eternally on the alert for moccasins. The vegetable layer was like a soft rubber sponge under our feet. It quivered on all sides of us when we moved, and was much too soft to allow us to spring out of the way of striking snakes. I did not make an exact count, but at least every fifteen minutes we discovered one of the reptiles coiled in our path. We walked around it and left it unmolested. Several times I glimpsed the tail of a snake disappearing into one of the grass mounds.

We had an uncomfortable experience late in the afternoon. I stumbled on a moccasin almost as large as my arm. It was shedding. The most vicious of all snakes in the western hemisphere is the water moccasin at the time it sheds its skin. Blind then, it will attack any noise and possibly heat. The snake charged us. Steve caught it expertly on the end of his pole and flung it thirty feet across the swamp. We could see the prairie moving where it thrashed around in the grass.

Twice Steve, who was heavier than I, broke through the false earth. Both times he flung his pole into a horizontal position and caught himself before he went out of sight.

An hour before complete darkness, we made our way to a lone couple of trees on the prairie, where the mound under the trunks stood several feet above the surrounding water. As we approached, I could see that the mounds were completely dry. It was a place where we could rest and sleep. Somehow the thought of fighting mosquitoes again all night no longer appalled me. I felt that if I could lie down somewhere out of the water, I would sleep a week. I stumbled forward, ready to fall on the dry earth, and Steve yanked at my arm.

"Watch it!"

I fell backward from force of habit and instinct rather than from quick thinking. A huge cottonmouth was coiled almost in front of my face. Why he didn't strike, I don't know. Perhaps the wilderness gods had relented momentarily.

From a distance we examined the mound of earth. Seven snakes were coiled upon it. We might have captured the mound with our poles, but could we have held it without a fire. The nearest clump of trees was at least a mile away, across the bog. The light was too dim for safe travel. Steve's voice was flat.

"We've come through tighter spots than this," he muttered, grimly.

Out on the marsh the breeze had died and the air was hot once more. The sun had gone completely, and from somewhere out of the infinite, the faint beat of drums started up again. I had the oppressed feeling that we were two inconsequential humans in the womb of all creation, and that the wilderness was pushing at us, crowding us down, trying to force us into the morass. Steve spoke between his teeth.

"We can't stay here. A hundred yards back the ground was a little firmer. We'll try it there."

We made our way cautiously to where the earth did not shake quite so much. In the darkness I expected any moment to tread on one of the big snakes, but it was a chance we had to take. I brushed wearily at the clouds of mosquitoes, and we put down the poles to support our weight on the quaking marsh. I lay down on the grass and covered my face in my arms. The swamp spun around and the drums were like pounding hammers in my ears.

I don't remember going to sleep. I awoke cold and cramped. My clothes were wet through from contact with the saturated earth and I was shivering. Wet clouds pressed down around us and drizzled on the marsh. The mosquitoes were gone. I tried to move an arm, but it wouldn't work. I turned it over with my other hand and it flopped back like a dead stick. I had probably slept on it half the night. I dragged my body into a sitting position.

"It's almost dawn," Steve said. "It's going to rain."

The mists turned gray, then white. With the arrival of daybreak, they lifted a little and rain sprinkled gently in our faces.

"If we don't get out today," Steve said, in a quiet voice, "we're probably through."

We stumbled southward. In a few minutes my body was warm again, but not the least refreshed, even from the sleep. I lost track of time and distance and space. I fell on my face and got up and weaved on again, like a drunk man. I hardly knew when we left the prairie and went into the woods. I remember pushing through vegetation so thick that when I fell the branches supported my weight. The yellow flies had caked my neck with blood. Anhingas flopped out of the trees like black spectres in front of us and flew off through the timber. We crossed a sandy spit of ground, the first dry land we had seen. I wanted to stop there, but Steve pushed us on.

We must have traveled on nerve the last half of the day. It was almost dark when we stumbled forward and fell into deep water at the edge of a cypress thicket. I thought it was another alligator hole, but Steve pulled me back into the wooded fringe.

"Billy Lake!" he said.

The sound of the word *Home* was never sweeter in my ears.

We pushed a log into the water and paddled across on it. We crawled out on that rotten pier we had left, what seemed a century ago. We staggered over the narrow runway and fell on the sandy bank that marked Jones Island landing. An hour later Lem, coming out of the swamp with two fishermen, found us there, sprawled in the sand, asleep.

Who doubts the statement that there's more to fishing than the fish. Not I, brother!

ALL GOLD CANYON

JACK LONDON

The thirst for gold—to "strike it rich"—turned ordinary men into survivalists in the great rush to the Yukon and Alaska of 1897–1899. More than 100,000 men are thought to have started the arduous journey to the Klondike, with 30,000 actually making it to the gold region. As witnessed by Jack London and captured in his amazing prose, the terrain and weather create dramas of life and death. If you've ever wondered what it would be like to be on your own, panning for gold in the vastness of the Yukon, you need look no further. This tale is so complete, you can follow this old timer's tracks step by step to learn how to not only survive but perhaps find a fortune in some pristine stream lost among the mountains.

■ ■ ■

It was the green heart of the canyon, where the walls swerved back from the rigid plan and relieved their harshness of line by making a little sheltered nook and filling it to the brim with sweetness and roundness and softness. Here all things rested. Even the narrow stream ceased its turbulent down-rush long enough to form a quiet pool. Knee-deep in the water, with drooping head and half-shut eyes, drowsed a red-coated, many-antlered buck.

On one side, beginning at the very lip of the pool, was a tiny meadow, a cool, resilient surface of green that extended to the base of the frowning wall. Beyond the pool a gentle slope of earth ran up and up to meet the opposing wall. Fine grass covered the slope—grass that was spangled with flowers, with here and there patches of color, orange and purple and golden. Below, the canyon was shut in. There was no view. The walls leaned together abruptly and the canyon ended in a chaos of rocks, moss-covered and hidden by a green screen of vines and creepers and boughs of trees. Up the canyon rose far hills and peaks, the big foothills, pine-covered and remote. And far beyond, like clouds upon the border of the slay, towered minarets of white, where the Sierra's eternal snows flashed austerely the blazes of the sun.

There was no dust in the canyon. The leaves and flowers were clean and virginal. The grass was young velvet. Over the pool three cottonwoods sent their scurvy fluffs fluttering down the quiet air. On the slope the blossoms of the wine-wooded manzanita filled the air with springtime odors, while the leaves, wise with experience, were already beginning their vertical twist against the coming aridity of summer. In the open spaces on the slope, beyond the farthest shadow-reach of the manzanita, poised the mariposa lilies, like so many flights of jewelled moths suddenly arrested and on the verge of trembling into flight again. Here and there that woods harlequin, the madrone, permitting itself to be caught in the act of changing its pea-green trunk to madder-red, breathed its fragrance into the air from great clusters of waxen bells. Creamy white were these bells, shaped like lilies-of-the-valley, with the sweetness of perfume that is of the springtime.

There was not a sigh of wind. The air was drowsy with its weight of perfume. It was a sweetness that would have been cloying had the air been heavy and humid. But the air was sharp and thin. It was as starlight transmuted into atmosphere, shot through and warmed by sunshine, and flower-drenched with sweetness.

An occasional butterfly drifted in and out through the patches of light and shade. And from all about rose the low and sleepy hum of mountain bees—feasting Sybarites that jostled one another good-naturedly at the board, nor found time for rough discourtesy. So quietly did the little stream drip and ripple its way through the canyon that it spoke only in faint and occasional gurgles. The voice of the stream was as a drowsy whisper, ever interrupted by dozings and silences, ever lifted again in the awakenings.

The motion of all things was a drifting in the heart of the canyon. Sunshine and butterflies drifted in and out among the trees. The hum of the bees and the whisper of the stream were a drifting of sound. And the drifting sound and drifting color seemed to weave together in the making of a delicate and intangible fabric which was the spirit of the place. It was a spirit of peace that was not of death, but of smooth-pulsing life, of quietude that was not silence, of movement that was not action, of repose that was quick with existence without being violent with struggle and travail. The spirit of the place was the spirit of the peace of the living, somnolent with the easement and content of prosperity, and undisturbed by rumors of far wars.

The red-coated, many-antlered buck acknowledged the lordship of the spirit of the place and dozed knee-deep in the cool, shaded pool. There seemed no flies to vex him and he was languid with rest. Sometimes his ears moved when the stream awoke and whispered; but they moved lazily, with, foreknowledge that it was merely the stream grown garrulous at discovery that it had slept.

But there came a time when the buck's ears lifted and tensed with swift eagerness for sound. His head was turned down the canyon. His sensitive, quivering nostrils scented the air. His eyes could not pierce the green screen through which the stream rippled away, but to his ears came the voice of a man. It was a steady, monotonous, singsong voice. Once the buck heard the harsh clash of metal upon rock. At the sound he snorted with a sudden start that jerked him through the air from water to meadow, and his feet sank into the young velvet, while he pricked his ears and again scented the air. Then he stole across the tiny meadow, pausing once and again to listen, and faded away out of the canyon like a wraith, soft-footed and without sound.

The clash of steel-shod soles against the rocks began to be heard, and the man's voice grew louder. It was raised in a sort of chant and became distinct with nearness, so that the words could be heard:

> *"Turn around an' tu'n yo' face*
> *Untoe them sweet hills of grace*
> *(D' pow'rs of sin yo' am scornin'!).*
> *Look about an' look aroun',*
> *Fling yo' sin-pack on d' groun'*
> *(Yo' will meet wid d' Lord in d' mornin'!)."*

A sound of scrambling accompanied the song, and the spirit of the place fled away on the heels of the red-coated buck. The green screen was burst asunder, and a man peered out at the meadow and the pool and the sloping side-hill. He was a deliberate sort of man. He took in the scene with one embracing glance, then ran his eyes over the details to verify the general impression. Then, and not until then, did he open his mouth in vivid and solemn approval:

"Smoke of life an' snakes of purgatory! Will you just look at that! Wood an' water an' grass an' a side-hill! A pocket-hunter's delight an' a cayuse's paradise! Cool green for tired eyes! Pink pills for pale people ain't in it. A secret pasture for prospectors and a resting-place for tired burros, by damn!"

He was a sandy-complexioned man in whose face geniality and humor seemed the salient characteristics. It was a mobile face, quick-changing to inward mood and thought. Thinking was in him a visible process. Ideas chased across his face like wind-flaws across the surface of a lake. His hair, sparse and unkempt of growth, was as indeterminate and colorless as his complexion. It would seem that all the color of his frame had gone into his eyes, for they were startlingly blue. Also, they were laughing and merry eyes, within them much of the naïveté and wonder of the child; and yet, in an unassertive way they contained much of calm self-reliance and strength of purpose founded upon self-experience and experience of the world.

From out the screen of vines and creepers he flung ahead of him a miner's pick and shovel and gold-pan. Then he crawled out himself into the open. He was clad in faded overalls and black cotton shirt, with hobnailed brogans on his feet, and on his head a hat whose shapelessness and stains advertised the rough usage of wind and rain and sun and camp-smoke. He stood erect, seeing wide-eyed the secrecy of the scene and sensuously inhaling the warm, sweet breath of the canyon-garden through nostrils that dilated and quivered with delight. His eyes narrowed to laughing slits of blue, his face wreathed itself in joy, and his mouth curled in a smile as he cried aloud:

"Jumping dandelions and happy hollyhocks, but that smells good to me! Talk about your attar o' roses an' cologne factories! They ain't in it!"

He had the habit of soliloquy. His quick-changing facial expressions might tell every thought and mood, but the tongue, perforce, ran hard after, repeating, like a second Boswell.

The man lay down on the lip of the pool and drank long and deep of its water. "Tastes good to me," he murmured, lifting his head and gazing across the pool at the side-hill, while he wiped his mouth with the back of his hand. The side-hill attracted his attention. Still lying on his stomach, he studied the hill formation long and carefully. It was a practised eye that travelled up the slope to the crumbling canyon-wall and back and down again to the edge of the pool. He scrambled to his feet and favored the side-hill with a second survey.

"Looks good to me," he concluded, picking up his pick and shovel and gold-pan.

He crossed the stream below the pool, stepping agilely from stone to stone. Where the side-hill touched the water he dug up a shovelful of dirt and put it into the gold-pan. He squatted down, holding the pan in his two hands, and partly immersing it in the stream. Then he imparted to the pan a deft circular motion that sent the water sluicing in and out through the dirt and gravel. The larger and the lighter particles worked to the surface, and these, by a skilful dipping movement of the pan, he spilled out and over the edge. Occasionally, to expedite matters, he rested the pan and with his fingers raked out the large pebbles and pieces of rock.

The contents of the pan diminished rapidly until only fine dirt and the smallest bits of gravel remained. At this stage he began to work very deliberately and carefully. It was fine washing, and he washed fine and finer, with a keen scrutiny and delicate and fastidious touch. At last the pan seemed empty of everything but water; but with a quick semicircular flirt that sent the water flying over the shallow rim into the stream, he disclosed a layer of black sand on the bottom of the pan. So thin was this layer that it was like a streak of paint. He examined it closely. In the midst of it was a tiny golden speck. He dribbled a little water in over the depressed edge of the pan. With a quick flirt he sent the water sluicing across the bottom, turning the grains of black sand over and over. A second tiny golden speck rewarded his effort.

The washing had now become very fine—fine beyond all need of ordinary placer-mining. He worked the black sand, a small portion at a time, up the shallow rim of the pan. Each small portion he examined sharply, so that his eyes saw every grain of it before he allowed it to slide over the edge and away. Jealously, bit by bit, he let the black sand slip away. A golden speck, no larger than a pin-point, appeared on the rim, and by his manipulation of the riveter it returned to the bottom of the tile pan. And in such fashion another speck was disclosed, and another. Great was his care of them. Like a shepherd he herded his flock of golden specks so that not one should be lost. At last, of the pan of dirt nothing remained but his golden herd. He counted it, and then, after all his labor, sent it flying out of the pan with one final swirl of water.

But his blue eyes were shining with desire as he rose to his feet. "Seven," he muttered aloud, asserting the sum of the specks for which he had toiled so hard and which he had so wantonly thrown away. "Seven," he repeated, with the emphasis of one trying to impress a number on his memory.

He stood still a long while, surveying the hill-side. In his eyes was a curiosity, new-aroused and burning. There was an exultance about his bearing and a keenness like that of a hunting animal catching the fresh scent of game.

He moved down the stream a few steps and took a second panful of dirt.

Again came the careful washing, the jealous herding of the golden specks, and the wantonness with which he sent them flying into the stream when he had counted their number.

"Five," he muttered, and repeated, "five."

He could not forbear another survey of the hill before filling the pan farther down the stream. His golden herds diminished. "Four, three, two, two, one," were his memory-tabulations as he moved down the stream. When but one speck of gold rewarded his washing, he stopped and built a fire of dry twigs. Into this he thrust the gold-pan and burned it till it was blue-black. He held up the pan and examined it critically. Then he nodded approbation. Against such a color-background he could defy the tiniest yellow speck to elude him.

Still moving down the stream, he panned again. A single speck was his reward. A third pan contained no gold at all. Not satisfied with this, he panned three times again, taking his shovels of dirt within a foot of one another. Each pan proved empty of gold, and the fact, instead of discouraging him, seemed to give him satisfaction. His elation increased with each barren washing, until he arose, exclaiming jubilantly:

"If it ain't the real thing, may God knock off my head with sour apples!"

Returning to where he had started operations, he began to pan up the stream. At first his golden herds increased—increased prodigiously. "Fourteen, eighteen, twenty-one, twenty-six," ran his memory tabulations. Just above the pool he struck his richest pan—thirty-five colors.

"Almost enough to save," he remarked regretfully as he allowed the water to sweep them away.

The sun climbed to the top of the sky. The man worked on. Pan by pan, he went up the stream, the tally of results steadily decreasing.

"It's just booful, the way it peters out," he exulted when a shovelful of dirt contained no more than a single speck of gold.

And when no specks at all were found in several pans, he straightened up and favored the hillside with a confident glance.

"Ah, ha! Mr. Pocket!" he cried out, as though to an auditor hidden somewhere above him beneath the surface of the slope. "Ah, ha! Mr. Pocket! I'm a-comin', I'm a-comin', an' I'm shorely gwine to get yer! You heah me, Mr. Pocket? I'm gwine to get yer as shore as punkins ain't cauliflowers!"

He turned and flung a measuring glance at the sun poised above him in the azure of the cloudless sky. Then he went down the canyon, following the line of shovel-holes he had made in filling the pans. He crossed the stream below the pool and disappeared through the green screen. There was little opportunity for the spirit of the place to return with its quietude and repose, for the man's voice, raised in ragtime song, still dominated the canyon with possession.

After a time, with a greater clashing of steel-shod feet on rock, he returned. The green screen was tremendously agitated. It surged back and forth in the throes of a struggle. There was a loud grating and clanging of metal. The man's voice leaped to a higher pitch and was sharp with imperativeness. A large body plunged and panted. There was a snapping and ripping and rending, and amid a shower of falling leaves a horse burst through the screen. On its back was a pack, and from this trailed broken vines and torn creepers. The animal gazed with astonished eyes at the scene into which it had been precipitated, then dropped its head to the grass and began contentedly to graze. A second horse scrambled into view, slipping once on the mossy rocks and regaining equilibrium when its hoofs sank into the yielding surface of the meadow. It was riderless, though on its back was a high-horned Mexican saddle, scarred and discolored by long usage.

The man brought up the rear. He threw off pack and saddle, with an eye to camp location, and gave the animals their freedom to graze. He unpacked his food and got out frying-pan and coffee-pot. He gathered an armful of dry wood, and with a few stones made a place for his fire.

My!" he said, "but I've got an appetite. I could scoff iron-filings an' horseshoe nails an' thank you kindly, ma'am, for a second helpin'."

He straightened up, and, while he reached for matches in the pocket of his overalls, his eyes travelled across the pool to the side-hill. His fingers had clutched the match-box, but they relaxed their hold and the hand came out empty. The man wavered perceptibly. He looked at his preparations for cooking and he looked at the hill.

"Guess I'll take another whack at her," he concluded, starting to cross the stream.

"They ain't no sense in it, I know," he mumbled apologetically. "But keepin' grub back an hour ain't goin' to hurt none, I reckon."

A few feet back from his first line of test-pans he started a second line. The sun dropped down the western sky, the shadows lengthened, but the man worked on. He began a third line of test-pans. He was cross-cutting the hillside, line by line, as he ascended. The centre of each line produced the richest pans, while the ends came where no colors showed in the pan. And as he ascended the hillside the lines grew perceptibly shorter. The regularity with which their length diminished served to indicate that somewhere up the slope the last line would be so short as to have scarcely length at all, and that beyond could come only a point. The design was growing into an inverted "V." The converging sides of this "V" marked the boundaries of the gold-bearing dirt.

The apex of the "V" was evidently the man's goal. Often he ran his eye along the converging sides and on up the hill, trying to divine the apex, the point where the gold-bearing dirt must cease. Here resided "Mr. Pocket"—for so the man familiarly addressed the imaginary point above him on the slope, crying out:

"Come down out o' that, Mr. Pocket! Be right smart an' agreeable, an' come down!"

"All right," he would add later, in a voice resigned to determination. "All right, Mr. Pocket. It's plain to me I got to come right up an' snatch you out bald-headed. An' I'll do it! I'll do it!" he would threaten still later.

Each pan he carried down to the water to wash, and as he went higher up the hill the pans grew richer, until he began to save the gold in an empty baking-powder can which he carried carelessly in his hip-pocket. So engrossed was he in his toil that he did not notice the long twilight of oncoming night. It was not until he tried vainly to see the gold colors in the bottom of the pan that he realized the passage of time. He straightened up abruptly. An expression of whimsical wonderment and awe overspread his face as he drawled:

"Gosh darn my buttons! If I didn't plumb forget dinner!"

He stumbled across the stream in the darkness and lighted his long-delayed fire. Flapjacks and bacon and warmed-over beans constituted his supper. Then he smoked a pipe by the smouldering coals, listening to the night noises and watching the moonlight stream through the canyon. After that he unrolled his bed, took off his heavy shoes, and pulled the blankets up to his chin. His face showed white in the moonlight, like the face of a corpse. But it was a corpse that knew its resurrection, for the man rose suddenly on one elbow and gazed across at his hillside.

"Good night, Mr. Pocket," he called sleepily. "Good night."

He slept through the early gray of morning until the direct rays of the sun smote his closed eyelids, when he awoke with a start and looked about him until he had established the continuity of his existence and identified his present self with the days previously lived.

To dress, he had merely to buckle on his shoes. He glanced at his fireplace and at his hillside, wavered, but fought down the temptation and started the fire.

"Keep yer shirt on, Bill; keep yer shirt on," he admonished himself. "What's the good of rushin'? No use in gettin' all het up an' sweaty. Mr. Pocket'll wait for you. He ain't a-runnin' away before you can get yer breakfast. Now, what you want, Bill, is something fresh in yer bill o' fare. So it's up to you to go an' get it."

He cut a short pole at the water's edge and drew from one of his pockets a bit of line and a draggled fly that had once been a royal coachman.

"Mebbe they'll bite in the early morning," he muttered, as he made his first cast into the pool. And a moment later he was gleefully crying: "What'd I tell you, eh? What'd I tell you?"

He had no reel, nor any inclination to waste time, and by main strength, and swiftly, he drew out of the water a flashing ten-inch trout. Three more, caught in rapid succession, furnished his breakfast. When he came to the stepping-stones on his way to his hillside, he was struck by a sudden thought, and paused.

"I'd just better take a hike down-stream a ways," he said. "There's no tellin' what cuss may be snoopin' around."

But he crossed over on the stones, and with a "I really oughter take that hike," the need of the precaution passed out of his mind and he fell to work.

At nightfall he straightened up. The small of his back was stiff from stooping toil, and as he put his hand behind him to soothe the protesting muscles, he said:

"Now what d'ye think of that, by damn? I clean forgot my dinner again! If I don't watch out, I'll sure be degenera-tin' into a two-meal-a-day crank."

"Pockets is the damnedest things I ever see for makin' a man absent-minded," he communed that night, as he crawled into his blankets. Nor did he forget to call up the hillside, "Good night, Mr. Pocket! Good night!"

Rising with the sun, and snatching a hasty breakfast, he was early at work. A fever seemed to be growing in him, nor did the increasing richness of the test-pans allay this fever. There was a flush in his cheek other than that made by the heat of the sun, and he was oblivious to fatigue and the passage of time. When he filled a pan with dirt, he ran down the hill to wash it; nor could he forbear running up the hill again, panting and stumbling profanely, to refill the pan.

He was now a hundred yards from the water, and the inverted "V" was assuming definite proportions. The width of the pay-dirt steadily decreased, and the man extended in his mind's eye the sides of the "V" to their meeting-place far up the hill. This was his goal, the apex of the "V," and he panned many times to locate it.

"Just about two yards above that manzanita bush an' a yard to the right," he finally concluded.

Then the temptation seized him. "As plain as the nose on your face," he said, as he abandoned his laborious cross-cutting and climbed to the indicated apex. He filled a pan and carried it down the hill to wash. It contained no trace of gold. He dug deep, and he dug shallow, filling and washing a dozen pans, and was unrewarded even by the tiniest golden speck. He was enraged at having yielded to the temptation, and cursed himself blasphemously and pridelessly. Then he went down the hill and took up the cross-cutting.

"Slow an' certain, Bill; slow an' certain," he crooned. "Short-cuts to fortune ain't in your line, an' it's about time you know it. Get wise, Bill; get wise. Slow an' certain's the only hand you can play; so go to it, an' keep to it, too."

As the cross-cuts decreased, showing that the sides of the "V" were converging, the depth of the " V " increased. The gold-trace was dipping into the hill. It was only at thirty inches beneath the surface that he could get colors in his pan. The dirt he found at twenty-five inches from the surface, and at thirty-five inches, yielded barren pans. At the base of the "V," by the water's edge, he had found the gold colors at the grass roots. The higher he went up the hill, the deeper the gold dipped.

To dig a hole three feet deep in order to get one test-pan was a task of no mean magnitude; while between the man and the apex intervened an untold number of such holes to be. "An' there's no tellin' how much deeper it'll pitch," he sighed, in a moment's pause, while his fingers soothed his aching back.

Feverish with desire, with aching back and stiffening muscles, with pick and shovel gouging and mauling the soft brown earth, the man toiled up the hill. Before him was the smooth slope, spangled with flowers and made sweet with their breath. Behind him was devastation. It looked like some terrible eruption breaking out on the smooth skin of the hill. His slow progress was like that of a slug, befouling beauty with a monstrous trail.

Though the dipping gold-trace increased the man's work, he found consolation in the increasing richness of the pans. Twenty cents, thirty cents, fifty cents, sixty cents, were the values of the gold found in the pans, and at nightfall he washed his banner pan, which gave him a dollar's worth of gold-dust from a shovelful of dirt.

"I'll just bet it's my luck to have some inquisitive cuss come buttin' in here on my pasture," he mumbled sleepily that night as he pulled the blankets up to his chin.

Suddenly he sat upright. "Bill!" he called sharply. "Now, listen to me, Bill; d'ye hear! It's up to you, to-morrow mornin', to mosey round an' see what you can see. Understand? Tomorrow morning, an' don't you forget it!"

He yawned and glanced across at his side-hill. "Good night, Mr. Pocket," he called.

In the morning he stole a march on the sun, for he had finished breakfast when its first rays caught him, and he was climbing the wall of the canyon where it crumbled away and gave footing. From the outlook at the top he found himself in the midst of loneliness. As far as he could see, chain after chain of mountains heaved themselves into his vision. To the east his eyes, leaping the miles between range and range and between many ranges, brought up at last against the white-peaked Sierras—the main crest, where the backbone of the Western world reared itself against the sky. To the north and south he could see more distinctly the cross-systems that broke through the main trend of the sea of mountains. To the west the ranges fell away, one behind the other, diminishing and fading into the gentle foothills that, in turn, descended into the great valley which he could not see.

And in all that mighty sweep of earth he saw no sign of man nor of the handiwork of man—save only the torn bosom of the hillside at his feet. The man looked long and carefully. Once, far down his own canyon, he thought he saw in the air a faint hint of smoke. He looked again and decided that it was the purple haze of the hills made dark by a convolution of the canyon wall at its back.

"Hey, you, Mr. Pocket!" he called down into the canyon. "Stand out from under! I'm a-comin', Mr. Pocket! I'm a-comin'!"

The heavy brogans on the man's feet made him appear clumsy-footed, but he swung down from the giddy height as lightly and airily as a mountain goat. A rock, turning under his foot on the edge of the precipice, did not disconcert him. He seemed to know the precise time required for the turn to culminate in disaster, and in the meantime he utilized the false footing itself for the momentary earth-contact necessary to carry him on into safety. Where the earth sloped so steeply that it was impossible to stand for a second upright, the man did not hesitate. His foot pressed the impossible surface for but a fraction of the fatal second and gave him the bound that carried him onward. Again, where even the fraction of a second's footing was out of the question, he would swing his body past by a moment's hand-grip on a jutting knob of rock, a crevice, or a pre-cariously rooted shrub. At last, with a wild leap and yell, he exchanged the face of the wall for an earth-slide and finished the descent in the midst of several tons of sliding earth and gravel.

His first pan of the morning washed out over two dollars in coarse gold. It was from the centre of the "V." To either side the diminution in the values of the pans was swift. His lines of cross-cutting holes were growing very short. The converging sides of the inverted "V" were only a few yards apart. Their meeting-point was only a few yards above him. But the pay-streak was dipping deeper and deeper into the earth. By early afternoon he was sinking the test-holes five feet before the pans could show the gold-trace.

For that matter, the gold-trace had become something more than a trace; it was a placer mine in itself, and the man resolved to come back after he had found the pocket and work over the ground. But the increasing richness of the pans began to worry him. By late afternoon the worth of the pans had grown to three and four dollars. The man scratched his head perplexedly and looked a few feet up the hill at the manzanita bush that marked approximately the apex of the "V." He nodded his head and said oracularly:

"It's one o' two things, Bill; one o' two things. Either Mr. Pocket's spilled himself all out an' down the hill, or else Mr. Pocket's that damned rich you maybe won't be able to carry him all away with you. And that'd be hell, wouldn't it, now?" He chuckled at contemplation of so pleasant a dilemma.

Nightfall found him by the edge of the stream his eyes wrestling with the gathering darkness over the washing of a five-dollar pan.

"Wisht I had an electric light to go on working," he said.

He found sleep difficult that night. Many times he composed himself and closed his eyes for slumber to overtake him; but his blood pounded with too strong desire, and as many times his eyes opened and he murmured wearily, "Wisht it was sun-up." Sleep came to him in the end, but his eyes were open with the first paling or the stars, and the gray of dawn caught him with breakfast finished and climbing the hillside in the direction of the secret abiding-place of Mr. Pocket.

The first cross-cut the man made, there was space for only three holes, so narrow had become the pay-streak and so close was he to the fountainhead of the golden stream he had been following for four days.

"Be ca'm, Bill; be ca'm," he admonished himself, as he broke ground for the final hole where the sides of the "V" had at last come together in a point.

"I've got the almighty cinch on you, Mr. Pocket, an' you can't lose me," he said many times as he sank the hole deeper and deeper.

Four feet, five feet, six feet, he dug his way down into the earth. The digging grew harder. His pick grated on broken rock. He examined the rock. "Rotten quartz," was his conclusion as, with the shovel, he cleared the bottom of the hole of loose dirt. He attacked the crumbling quartz with the pick, bursting the disintegrating rock asunder with every stroke.

He thrust his shovel into the loose mass. His eye caught a gleam of yellow. He dropped the shovel and squatted suddenly on his heels. As a farmer rubs the clinging earth from fresh-dug potatoes, so the man, a piece of rotten quartz held in both hands, rubbed the dirt away.

"Sufferin' Sardanopolis!" he cried. "Lumps an' chunks of it! Lumps an' chunks of it!"

It was only half rock he held in his hand. The other half was virgin gold. He dropped it into his pan and examined another piece. Little yellow was to be seen, but with his strong fingers he crumbled the rotten quartz away till both hands were filled with glowing yellow. He rubbed the dirt away from fragment after fragment, tossing them into the gold-pan. It was a treasure-hole. So much had the quartz rotted away that there was less of it than there was of gold. Now and again he found a piece to which no rock clung—a piece that was all gold. A chunk, where the pick had laid open the heart of the gold, glittered like a handful of yellow jewels, and he cocked his head at it and slowly turned it around and over to observe the rich play of the light upon it.

"Talk about yer Too Much Gold diggin's!" the man snorted contemptuously. "Why, this diggin' 'd make it look like thirty cents. This diggin' is All Gold. An' right here an' now I name this yere canyon 'All Gold Canyon,' b' gosh!"

Still squatting on his heels, he continued examining the fragments and tossing them into the pan. Suddenly there came to him a premonition of danger. It seemed a shadow had fallen upon him. But there was no shadow. His heart had given a great jump up into his throat and was choking him. Then his blood slowly chilled and he felt the sweat of his shirt cold against his flesh.

He did not spring up nor look around. He did not move. He was considering the nature of the premonition he had received, trying to locate the source of the mysterious force that had warned him, striving to sense the imperative presence of the unseen thing that threatened him. There is an aura of things hostile, made manifest by messengers refined for the senses to know; and this aura he felt, but knew not how he felt it. His was the feeling as when a cloud passes over the sun. It seemed that between him and life had passed something dark and smothering and menacing; a gloom, as it were, that swallowed up life and made for death—his death.

Every force of his being impelled him to spring up and confront the unseen danger, but his soul dominated the panic, and he remained squatting on his heels, in his hands a chunk of gold. He did not dare to look around, but he knew by now that there was something behind him and above him. He made believe to be interested in the gold in his hand. He examined it critically, turned it over and over, and rubbed the dirt from it. And all the time he knew that something behind him was looking at the gold over his shoulder.

Still feigning interest in the chunk of gold in his hand, he listened intently and he heard the breathing of the thing behind him. His eyes searched the ground in front of him for a weapon, but they saw only the uprooted gold, worthless to him now in his extremity. There was his pick, a handy weapon on occasion; but this was not such an occasion. The man realized his predicament. He was in a narrow hole that was seven feet deep. His head did not come to the surface of the ground. He was in a trap.

He remained squatting on his heels. He was quite cool and collected; but his mind, considering every factor, showed him only his helplessness. He continued rubbing the dirt from the quartz fragments and throwing the gold into the pan. There was nothing else for him to do. Yet he knew that he would have to rise up, sooner or later, and face the danger that breathed at his back.

The minutes passed, and with the passage of each minute he knew that by so much he was nearer the time when he must stand up, or else—and his wet shirt went cold against his flesh again at the thought—or else he might receive death as he stooped there over his treasure.

Still he squatted on his heels, rubbing dirt from gold and debating in just what manner he should rise up. He might rise up with a rush and claw his way out of the hole to meet whatever threatened on the even footing above ground. Or he might rise up slowly and carelessly, and feign casually to discover the thing that breathed at his back. His instinct and every fighting fibre of his body favored the mad, clawing rush to the surface. His intellect, and the craft thereof, favored the slow and cautious meeting with the thing that menaced and which he could not see. And while he debated, a loud, crashing noise burst on his ear. At the same instant he received a stunning blow on the left side of the back, and from the point of impact felt a rush of flame through his flesh. He sprang up in the air, but halfway to his feet collapsed. His body crumpled in like a leaf withered in sudden heat, and he came down, his chest across his pan of gold, his face in the dirt and rock, his legs tangled and twisted because of the restricted space at the bottom of the hole. His legs twitched convulsively several times. His body was shaken as with a mighty ague. There was a slow expansion of the lungs, accompanied by a deep sigh. Then the air was slowly, very slowly, exhaled, and his body as slowly flattened itself down into inertness.

Above, revolver in hand, a man was peering down over the edge of the hole. He peered for a long time at the prone and motionless body beneath him. After a while the stranger sat down on the edge of the hole so that he could see into it, and rested the revolver on his knee. Reaching his hand into a pocket, he drew out a wisp of brown paper. Into this he dropped a few crumbs of tobacco. The combination became a cigarette, brown and squat, with the ends turned in. Not once did he take his eyes from the body at the bottom of the hole. He lighted the cigarette and drew its smoke into his lungs with a caressing intake of the breath. He smoked slowly. Once the cigarette went out and he relighted it. And all the while he studied the body beneath him.

In the end he tossed the cigarette stub away and rose to his feet. He moved to the edge of the hole. Spanning it, a hand resting on each edge, and with the revolver still in the right hand, he muscled his body down into the hole. While his feet were yet a yard from the bottom he released his hands and dropped down.

At the instant his feet struck bottom he saw the pocket-miner's arm leap out, and his own legs knew a swift, jerking grip that overthrew him. In the nature of the jump his revolver-hand was above his head. Swiftly as the grip had flashed about his legs, just as swiftly he brought the revolver down. He was still in the air, his fall in process of completion, when he pulled the trigger. The explosion was deafening in the confined space. The smoke filled the hole so that he could see nothing. He struck the bottom on his back, and like a cat's the pocket-miner's body was on top of him. Even as the miner's body passed on top, the stranger crooked in his right arm to fire; and even in that instant the miner, with a quick trust of elbow, struck his wrist. The muzzle was thrown up and the bullet thudded into the dirt of the side of the hole.

The next instant the stranger felt the miner's hand grip his wrist. The struggle was now for the revolver. Each man strove to turn it against the other's body. The smoke in the hole was clearing. The stranger, lying on his back, was beginning to see dimly. But suddenly he was blinded by a handful of dirt deliberately flung into his eyes by his antagonist. In that moment of shock his grip on the revolver was broken. In the next moment he felt a smashing darkness descend upon his brain, and in the midst of the darkness even the darkness ceased.

But the pocket-miner fired again and again, until the revolver was empty. Then he tossed it from him and, breathing heavily, sat down on the dead man's legs.

The miner was sobbing and struggling for breath. "Measly skunk!" he panted; "a-campin' on my trail an' lettin' me do the work, an' then shootin' me in the back!"

He was half crying from anger and exhaustion. He peered at the face of the dead man. It was sprinkled with loose dirt and gravel, and it was difficult to distinguish the features.

"Never laid eyes on him before," the miner concluded his scrutiny. "Just a common an' ordinary thief, damn him! An' he shot me in the back! He shot me in the back!"

He opened his shirt and felt himself, front and back, on his left side.

"Went clean through, and no harm done!" he cried jubilantly. "I'll bet he aimed right all right, but he drew the gun over when he pulled the trigger—the cuss! But I fixed 'm! Oh, I fixed 'm!"

His fingers were investigating the bullet-hole in his side, and a shade of regret passed over his face. "It's goin' to be stiffer'n hell," he said. "An' it's up to me to get mended an' get out o' here."

He crawled out of the hole and went down the hill to his camp. Half an hour later he returned, leading his packhorse. His open shirt disclosed the rude bandages with which he had dressed his wound. He was slow and awkward with his left-hand movements, but that did not prevent his using the arm.

The bight of the pack-rope under the dead man's shoulders enabled him to heave the body out of the hole. Then he set to work gathering up his gold. He worked steadily for several hours, pausing often to rest his stiffening shoulder and to exclaim:

"He shot me in the back, the measly skunk! He shot me in the back!"

When his treasure was quite cleaned up and wrapped securely into a number of blanket-covered parcels, he made an estimate of its value.

"Four hundred pounds, or I'm a Hottentot," he concluded. "Say two hundred in quartz an' dirt—that leaves two hundred pounds of gold. Bill! Wake up! Two hundred pounds of gold! Forty thousand dollars! An' it's yourn—all yourn!"

He scratched his head delightedly and his fingers blundered into an unfamiliar groove. They quested along it for several inches. It was a crease through his scalp where the second bullet had ploughed.

He walked angrily over to the dead man.

"You would, would you?" he bullied. "You would, eh? Well, I fixed you good an' plenty, an' I'll give you decent burial, too. That's more'n you'd have done for me."

He dragged the body to the edge of the hole and toppled it in. It struck the bottom with a dull crash, on its side, the face twisted up to the light. The miner peered down at it.

"An' you shot me in the back!" he said accusingly.

With pick and shovel he filled the hole. Then he loaded the gold on his horse. It was too great a load for the animal, and when he had gained his camp he transferred part of it to his saddle-horse. Even so, he was compelled to abandon a portion of his outfit—pick and shovel and gold-pan, extra food and cooking utensils, and divers odds and ends.

The sun was at the zenith when the man forced the horses at the screen of vines and creepers. To climb the huge boulders the animals were compelled to uprear and struggle blindly through the tangled mass of vegetation. Once the saddle-horse fell heavily and the man removed the pack to get the animal on its feet. After it started on its way again the man thrust his head out from among the leaves and peered up at the hillside.

"The measly skunk!" he said, and disappeared.

There was a ripping and tearing of vines and boughs. The trees surged back and forth, marking the passage of the animals through the midst of them. There was a clashing of steel-shod hoofs on stone, and now and again an oath or a sharp cry of command. Then the voice of the man was raised in song:—

"Tu'n around an' tu'n yo' face
Untoe them sweet hills of grace
(D' pow'rs of sin yo' am scornin'!).
Look about an, look aroun',
Fling yo' sin-pack on d' groun'
(Yo' will meet wid d' Lord in d' mornin'!)."

The song grew faint and fainter, and through the silence crept back the spirit of the place. The stream once more drowsed and whispered; the hum of the mountain bees rose sleepily. Down through the perfume-weighted air fluttered the snowy fluffs of the cottonwoods. The butterflies drifted in and out among the trees, and over all blazed the quiet sunshine. Only remained the hoof-marks in the meadow and the torn hillside to mark the boisterous trail of the life that had broken the peace of the place and passed on.

BENDING THE MAP
LAURENCE GONZALES

I first became acquainted with the engaging prose of Laurence Gonzales with his book One Zero Charlie, *an illuminating account of the world of general aviation. Since then I have followed his work through other books and articles, but none have been more hard hitting than his book* Deep Survival. *Boasting two subtitles, one reads, "Who Lives, Who Dies and Why"; the other, "True Stories of Miraculous Endurance and Sudden Death." As these descriptions of the book promise,* Deep Survival *takes us into situations we may hope to never encounter but love reading about. Our outdoor hikes, or climbs, or river-running trips may start as simple, enjoyable challenges, but they can quickly turn into a fight to stay alive. In this true tale set in Colorado's Rocky Mountain National Park, a strong young man, a firefighter, experienced in hiking and climbing, faces such a fight. Laurence Gonzales shows us, moment by moment, how a trek into the mountains for pleasure can turn into a survival challenge. When you hit the trail with Gonzales in print, you will be arming yourself with strong lore on staying alive in the mountains.*

■ ■ ■

When Ken Killip set out on the trail at Milner Pass in Rocky Mountain National Park at dawn on August 8, 1998, he had the nagging sense that he should not have come. A group of friends had planned the three-day backcountry hiking and fishing trip, but the others had gradually dropped out until only Killip and his friend John York were left. Killip, a firefighter, wondered if he should drop out, too, but decided to

133

go ahead with the trip. From the trailhead, their route would follow the Continental Divide south for four miles, climbing 2,000 feet to the top of Mount Ida. There, at an altitude of 12,889 feet, they'd turn east, descend into the Gorge Lakes drainage, and hike two miles to Rock Lake. While six miles doesn't sound like much, hiking with a full pack to nearly 13,000 feet is serious business. In addition, Rock Lake sits at the edge of Forest Canyon, a densely wooded wilderness in the Big Thompson River valley. And as the local district ranger would later say, "It's one of the most remote areas in the park. It's pretty unforgiving."

Killip had plenty of outdoor experience. He had been with the Parker Fire Protection District just south of Denver for twenty-four years. He'd even had some survival training in the military. But Killip had never been in a place quite so rugged as this. And now the terrain, the altitude, and the heavy pack were taking their toll. He'd already given the tent to York to carry. York, a fellow firefighter and strong out-doorsman, repeatedly had to wait for Killip to catch up, and after five or six hours of that, York grew impatient and left Killip to fend for himself. Mismatching the abilities of people in the outdoors is a sure way to get into trouble. People routinely fail to realize that they have to travel at the speed of the slowest member, not the fastest.

Killip had been following York, who had been there before and knew the way. And although Killip had the map, York had the compass. They'd begun on a trail, but beyond the top of Mount Ida, it was a trailless wilderness, where you need both map and compass. Now, as he watched York disappear into the approaching weather, Killip didn't comprehend the insidious processes that were taking place. The world, though constantly changing, was the same as it had always been. The processes that would betray Killip were all taking place inside of him.

One type of mental model people form is a mental map: literally, a schematic of an area or a route. Killip had formed a sort of stochastic mental map of where he'd been since leaving his car. Because he'd been following York, he had not been checking his topographical map, and that is not a good way to create a reliable mental map. Now his brain was unconsciously trying to form a mental map of the route from a position he didn't really know to a destination he'd never seen before. That futile struggle contributed to his ill-defined anxiety.

In addition, a storm was rolling in, and Killip did not want to be the tallest object on the ridge. The area is well known for its afternoon lightning strikes. He decided to wait on the slope below the ridge until the thunderstorm passed. The multiple stresses of weather, fatigue, altitude, dehydration, and anxiety were closing in on Killip's ability to find that vital balance between useful emotion and reason.

As the storm began booming and flashing around him, it increased his level of stress. Killip had time to reflect on his misgivings about the trip, but his thinking was already beyond detailed, accurate analysis. In addition, stress was eroding his ability to perceive. He saw less, began to miss important cues from his environment.

Four day-hikers came off the trail to join him and wait out the rain. They told Killip that they'd seen his friend. Grasping at the wished-for reality, Killip concluded that all he'd have to do was hurry on ahead, and he'd find York. When at last the lightning stopped, Killip pressed on in a driving rain, intent on salvaging the trip.

He was climbing a steep slope that he was sure must be Mount Ida—it just had to be. He'd been walking all day under his heavy pack. He knew he would soon get to head down toward a cool, clear river with a string of jewel-like lakes. He could drink. The perception that he was climbing Mount Ida gave a more settled feeling to the area of his brain that was trying to create a mental map. At last, the hippocampus had something to work with. Killip could picture Mount Ida and its relationship to his destination, and mental maps are images. Without images, we are lost.

He'd been in motion for more than twelve hours. It was after 5:00 p.m., and he'd drunk the last of his water at about two o'clock. The sun was going down; the temperature was dropping. The rain continued to torment him.

When Killip struggled to the top, he turned east and began the descent into the drainage, following his image of where Rock Lake should be. But he immediately knew that something was wrong: There was an unpleasant jolt from the amygdala. This was not the place. The river and the little lakes and the rock shelf that York had told him he would see weren't there. The image and the world didn't match.

Killip had not, in fact, reached the summit of Mount Ida. He was looking instead down a parallel drainage about a mile to the north. Killip now teetered on the invisible dividing line between two worlds: He was in a state of only minor geographical confusion. He could have retraced his steps. He still had a grip on one route, but he didn't have the big picture. He knew what was behind him. He did not know what was ahead of him. He could see into his past, but he had lost that vital cortical ability to perceive the world and therefore to see into his own future.

· · ·

Psychologists who study the behavior of people who get lost report that very few ever backtrack. (The eyes look forward into real or imagined worlds.) In Killip's case, there were other factors, too. He'd walked all day, exhausted, dehydrated, cold, and wet, probably by now feeling like a fool in York's eyes. He'd come a very long way, and his gut told him that it would be a long and painful way back, which would not lead to water. Rock Lake (and rest and water) had to be close at hand. If he'd been able to reason more clearly, he could have understood that he was not on the route to Rock Lake. But logic was rapidly being pushed into the background by emotion and stress. So, by the simple act of putting one foot in front of the other, he was about to cross over from mild geographical confusion to a state of being genuinely lost.

Edward Cornell, one of the scientists who study the behavior of people who become lost, is a professor of psychology at the University of Alberta in Edmonton. "Being lost is a universal human condition," he told me. "But there is a very fuzzy area between being lost and not lost."

Until about half a century ago, there was a widespread belief among scientists that people had some sort of inherent sense of direction. The observation that certain peoples around the world were especially skilled at navigation in the absence of obvious cues was evidence for a magnetic sense. The Australian Aborigines and the Puluwat Islanders in the South Pacific were examples of peoples who seemed inexplicably good at navigating. But when they studied those peoples more closely, researchers realized that they had simply been trained from childhood to pick up very subtle cues from the environment and use them the way anyone else would use landmarks to find a route. Even those people can and do get lost. And after half a century of research, it turns out that their greatest skill lay in keeping an up-to-date mental map of their environment.

There is no agreement among scientists on an exact definition of being lost. William G. Syrotuck, a pioneer in the field, defined it as being the subject of a land search. But many land searches are initiated for people who are just not where they're supposed to be. Kenneth Hill, a teacher and psychologist who also manages search and rescue operations in Nova Scotia, built on Syrotuck's work. He defines being lost as "30 minutes of not knowing where you are." That would suggest that a number of pilots I know have been lost in local taverns. Scientists who study human spatial cognition define being lost as being unable to relate your position in space to known locations. But being lost includes a whole range of emotional and behavioral consequences as well.

Syrotuck was the first search and rescue expert to conduct systematic research on the behavior of people who become lost in the wilderness. In *Lost Person Behavior*, he writes that they tend to panic. "Panic usually implies tearing around or thrashing through the brush, but in its earlier stages it is less frantic. . . . It all starts when they look about and find that a supposedly familiar location now appears totally strange, or when they start to realize that it seems to be taking longer to reach a particular place than they had expected. There is a tendency to hurry to 'find the right place.' 'Maybe it's just over that little ridge.'"

Recent research in neuroscience has shed some light on how people navigate. The way we know where we are is complex, as are the parts of the brain we use—the hippocampus and its component parts (such as the subiculum, the entorhinal cortex, and CA-3 and CA-1 formations). Joseph LeDoux calls the hippocampus "a spatial cognition machine." Neuroscientists have described how the brain creates mental maps of the environment. Early research with rats in the 1970s by John O'Keefe at McGill University, among others, provided the first neurophysiological evidence that the hippocampus creates "a spatial reference map" in the brain. In addition, there are cells that fire depending on the position of the head and others that track the position of the whole body or its parts. Still other cells fire only when traveling in one direction.

O'Keefe more or less accidentally found what he called "place cells" in the rat hippocampus. Place cells are individual neurons that get mapped to fire when the animal is at a specific place. Normally, hippocampal cells fire perhaps only once every second on average. But at that mapped place, they fire hundreds of times faster. In tests with monkeys at the University of Oxford, cells were found that fired only when the animal was looking at a certain view. A single cell can map more than one place.

So there is an elaborate system involving the hippocampus and other areas of the brain for creating an analog of the world and your motion, position, and direction of travel within it. It works in concert with other systems to locate you in your mind. For example, through information from the inner ear (the vestibular system), your brain is constantly telling you whether you're upright or not and whether you're leaning over or falling backward. Through the proprioceptive system, the brain is constantly reading signals from nerve cells throughout the body to tell you where the parts of your body are. That's why you can touch your nose with your eyes closed. Without those systems, you'd get lost every time you tried to go anywhere, as experimental animals do when researchers destroy the hippocampal area of the brain. Alzheimer's patients do, too.

Place cells and other cells involved in navigation are constantly being reprogrammed. It's called "remapping." Any time you go to a new place, the brain begins trying to create a new map. For some people, it takes only one trip; others have to repeat the route several times to remember it. (We've all had the experience of waking in a strange place and not knowing where we are.) The hippocampus is associated with memory, and the maps appear to be stored in the same way as memory. You create not just routes but maps of areas of your environment, such as a room, your house, or your whole neighborhood. Many people find, for example, that they can easily navigate around their own bedroom or even large parts of their house without the lights on, because the mental map in their brain matches the real world. Blind people often get around just fine because they have excellent mental maps. Place cells in rats fire in the dark. But stress interferes with the work of the hippocampus, making it harder to make and revise your mental maps.

Interestingly, the hippocampus, which tells you where you are and where you're going (if the map is right), does not control the seeking of a goal. The urge to get to a specific place, the drive toward a goal, appears to be emotional. That makes sense, since the amygdala helps trigger action, especially as it relates to survival. Rats who have had the lateral nucleus of the amygdala destroyed lose their drive to get to a particular place. So, place and motivation are integrally connected, which may explain what keeps people moving when it would be safer for them to stay still.

When a person goes from a city to, say, Rocky Mountain National Park, it puts some unusual demands on the brain. In the city, all the visual cues are near and limited in number as well. You may see the inside of your home, the inside of your office, streets bordered by buildings, and so on. Rarely do most people get a sweeping panorama in a city. When you travel to the mountains, suddenly all the cues are different, as are all the requirements of mapping that are going on continuously and unconsciously in the brain. The brain is reaching out through the senses, bringing information in, attempting to grasp the environment and wire up a map. The input and output of the hippocampus and other areas are being sent to the amygdala to establish a drive toward beneficial things and an aversion to harmful things. The amygdala is set to respond with action. For a person displaced from his normal environment, the task of mapping the unfamiliar and vast world might feel a bit overwhelming.

■　■　■

So, with reason pretty much out of the picture and emotion driving hard toward survival strategies, Killip started down the wrong drainage as darkness and rain fell around him. It was the absence of a mental map of the place in which he found himself that caused the amygdala to begin sending danger signals. People recognize as good such places as the location of food, water, and members of the opposite sex. That's a primary task of adaptation and survival. People also recognize dangerous places. And it makes perfect sense that a dangerous place to be is one for which you have no mental map, for then you'd be unable to find food, water, or a mate.

Killip's seemingly irrational behavior makes sense when viewed from the brain's point of view. The fact of not having a mental map, of trying to create one in an environment where the sensory input made no sense, is interpreted as an emergency and triggers a physical (i.e., emotional) response. In the emergency of being no place, Killip's action makes sense to the organism, even though it later seems illogical. The organism needed him to hurry up and try to get some place quickly, a place that matched his mental map, a place that would provide access to the essentials of survival. This impulse explains Syrotuck's observation that people panic when they become lost. It gives a working definition of being lost: the inability to make the mental map match the environment.

So it was that Killip found himself blundering through dense timber in total darkness with the creepy feeling of knowing that he was nowhere. A chance flicker of lightning ignited reflections on a pond. Parched with thirst, Killip headed for it. He drank his fill and prepared to spend the night. He had no choice now. But he wasn't thinking straight. He had food in his pack, but York had the tent. Killip had garbage bags but didn't use them for a makeshift shelter. Although he needed a fire, wanted its warmth and light, he knew that open fires weren't permitted in this part of the park. As a firefighter, he felt he ought to follow that rule. (If he had made a fire, he might have been seen and rescued sooner.)

When a bear appeared, Killip got up and charged the animal, waving his jacket at it and shouting. The bear went away. Then Killip wondered what would have happened if he'd been injured so far from help.

He was able to heat a meal on his camp stove. Then he fell asleep.

When he awoke, he felt somewhat refreshed. But he would not recover from his fatigue and confusion that quickly. He still had the option of retracing his steps to his car. He could go back up the drainage. But he felt that he could not simply leave York and spoil the trip. York would be thinking: What a nitwit. And anyway, Killip didn't yet quite believe that he was lost.

Admitting that you are lost is difficult because having no mental map, being no place, is like having no self: It's impossible to conceive, because one of the main jobs of the organism is to adjust itself to place. That's why small children, when asked if they are lost, will say, "No, my Mommy is lost." The sense is: I'm not lost; I'm right here. But without a mental map, the organism can't go about its business and rapidly deteriorates. So to Killip, it seemed that he wasn't lost. Rock Lake was lost. It had to be just around the corner somewhere. Then everything would be all right. He had a firefighter's can-do persistence and a lost person's tendency to form a strategy, albeit a faulty one.

He began bushwhacking through forest so dense he sometimes had to remove his backpack to squeeze between the trees. It didn't occur to him that this might be a bad sign. But anytime you find yourself thinking it's easier to go around a mountain than over one, you know there's trouble upstairs.

As Syrotuck writes, "If things get progressively more unfamiliar and mixed up, [the victim] may then develop a feeling of vertigo, the trees and slopes seem to be closing in and a feeling of claustrophobia compels them to try to 'break out.' This is the point at which running or frantic scrambling may occur," as the organism frantically attempts to get a fix on an alien environment.

By afternoon, Killip's wanderings had severed all connection to the world he'd known. His circle of confusion had expanded so that he could no longer even retrace his steps: He was profoundly lost. And while the rational part of his brain remained convinced that he was getting close to Rock Lake, the emotional part was driving him on with more and more urgency. (He'd eventually pass within a quarter mile of Rock Lake, but not that day.)

As his brain continued the unconscious search for any cue with which to establish a mental map, the alarm signals grew more and more urgent: No place. No food. No people. *Get there, get there*, a voice seemed to say. *Hurry, hurry.*

Killip began scrambling up a steep scree slope to get a better view. Maybe if he just got up high . . . if he could just see the whole area, then everything would snap back into focus and he could calm down.

About halfway up, he lost his footing and couldn't self-arrest. He began to cartwheel down the long grade. When he came to a stop, he had suffered severely pulled muscles in his shoulder, ligament and cartilage damage in his knees, and two sprained ankles. He was lucky it wasn't fatal, as such a violent fall often is.

Killip dragged himself to a small pond, where he had no choice but to remain through another rainy night. He tried to reason, but something was wrong. He was cold and hurt but still believed he was forbidden from making a fire. He didn't even erect a shelter.

Killip awoke in pain and frustration. He'd had it with

trying to find Rock Lake. He was definitely going back to the car, he decided. Although he had no idea what direction to go, because he didn't know where he was, he began limping through the forest, battering his way through the trees, wasting precious energy. But with no understanding of what was happening to him, he could not settle down. Once again, he decided that the best strategy was to climb up and see if he could get an overall view of where he was.

As Syrotuck put it, "If they do not totally exhaust or injure themselves during outright panic, they may eventually get a grip on themselves and decide on some plan of action. What they decide to do may appear irrational to a calm observer, but does not seem nearly so unreasonable to the lost person who is now totally disoriented. Generally, they would be wiser and safer to stay put and get as comfortable and warm as possible, but many feel compelled to push on, urged by subconscious feelings." Urged on by the frustrating task that his unconscious brain activity had been trying to complete for so long now without success. The organism's main task is to map the self, map the environment, and keep the two in harmonious balance. Without the balance, the organism dies.

Killip began struggling up another steep and rocky slope. It was actually Terra Tomah Mountain, a 12,718-foot peak. But before he could get himself rim-rocked, a storm blew in and forced him back down toward the trees. He felt woozy. He felt strange. He knew he was in serious trouble, but there didn't seem to be anything he could do about it. He passed out with one arm slung around a tree trunk to keep himself from sliding down the steep rock.

It was past midnight when he awoke, wet and shaking uncontrollably. He looked around. The world was strange.

Everything was white. After a moment, he realized what he was seeing: Hailstones covered the ground to a depth of 12 inches. He had slept through a big storm.

When he'd set out on August 8, Killip had been a healthy, competent, well-equipped hiker. His pack contained everything he needed to survive at least a week in the wild. Now, just over two days after taking a wrong turn off the Continental Divide, he was huddled on an icy mountainside, exhausted, hungry, badly dehydrated, injured, and dangerously hypothermic. What had begun as a small error in navigation had progressed, step by innocent step, to a grim struggle for survival.

.   .   .

Syrotuck analyzed 229 search and rescue cases (11 percent of them fatal) and concluded that almost three quarters of those who died perished within the first forty-eight hours of becoming lost. Those who die can do so surprisingly quickly, and hypothermia is usually the official cause. Hypothermia is frighteningly insidious, but in some cases people just give up.

Anyone can get lost. I know. I have. But surprisingly few are genuinely prepared to live through the experience. I was staying at Many Glacier Hotel, in Glacier National Park, and decided to hike the half-hour nature trail with a friend before breakfast. But there was the air, and the view, and that spicy juniper smell of the mountains. There were those dizzying spaces and the Hansel and Gretel forest beckoning . . . Our experience of a week of hard hiking deep in the Montana wilderness had convinced us both that we knew our way around. We were fit and confident.

We left the little loop trail and followed a sign for Grinnell Lake. We took one fork, then another, then another.

When the first drops of rain started falling, we slipped into our cheap gift-shop ponchos and hurried on with a growing sense of urgency. We didn't consider turning back.

At last, we stood on the shore of a lake, trying to remember why it had seemed so important to get there. The soft hissing of rain suddenly accelerated to a clattering of hailstones. I looked over at my companion and saw that her face was pale and blotchy. Her teeth had begun to chatter. I felt a cold dread set like plaster in my stomach as the realization hit me that we were standing in a hailstorm, dressed in cotton T-shirts and garbage bags, at least two hours from home with no map or compass. *What were we thinking?*

We took off down the trail at a dead run, but when we reached a fork, she went one way and I went the other. We turned back to look at each other in horrified amazement. We had no idea which way we'd come. We finally chose one of the paths and had just set foot on it when we heard a human voice. We surged toward it, crashing through a few yards of dense forest, and found ourselves at a dock on another lake, where a tourist boat had just pulled up. Ice had already covered the windshield.

As we clambered aboard, we were told that it was the last boat of the day. I still sometimes wake up at night wondering what it would have been like if we had stayed on that path (which led deeper into the wilderness, as we later discovered from a glance at the map we'd left at the hotel) with no water, no fire, and no warm clothing, in what turned out to be a two-day ice storm.

In just a few hours, we'd gone from being carefree day hikers to panicked victims, saved only by dumb luck. Until that day in Glacier, I would not have believed how easily

I could get lost or how quickly I could lose my ability to reason.

One of Kenneth Hill's experiments involves taking a group of his students into a small forest in Nova Scotia. "It's about the size of a large city park," he told me, "and notorious for its maze of poorly marked trails." He leads the students in and then asks them to lead him out. Only one person has ever succeeded. "If you ask hikers on a trail to point out where they are on a map at any given moment," Hill said, "they are usually wrong."

In daily life, people operate on the necessary illusion that they know where they are. Most of the time, they don't. The only time most people are not lost to some degree is when they are at home. It's quite possible to know the route from one place to another without knowing precisely where you are. That's why streets have signs. Nevertheless, most people normally have enough route knowledge to get them where they're going. If they don't—as in my case, and in Ken Killip's case—they get lost.

It's simple. All you have to do is fail to update your mental map and then persist in following it even when the landscape (or your compass) tries to tell you it's wrong. Edward Cornell once told me, "Whenever you start looking at your map and saying something like, 'Well, that lake could have dried up,' or, 'That boulder could have moved,' a red light should go off. You're trying to make reality conform to your expectations rather than seeing what's there. In the sport of orienteering, they call that 'bending the map.'"

Killip was bending the map when he headed down the wrong drainage despite ample evidence that he was starting from the wrong place. But it's understandable how urgent it feels to make your mental map and the world conform. It's the essence of what every organism does, even those that don't have cognition as we know it.

If we persist in bending the map until we can no longer deny the evidence of our senses, it can be terrifying. "It's not something that happens immediately," Hill said. "First, it's a sense of disorientation: 'Uh-oh, I'm not in Kansas anymore.' Then the woods start to become strange; landmarks are no longer familiar."

Since the organism's survival depends on a reasonable match between mental map and environment, as the two diverge, the hippocampus spins its wheels and the amygdala sends out alarm signals even as the motivational circuits urge you on and on. The result is vertigo, claustrophobia, panic, and wasted motion. Since most people aren't conscious of the process, there's no way to reflect on what's happening. All you know is that it feels as if you're going mad. (And what else is insanity but a failure to match mind and world?) When at last the full weight of the incongruity hits you, the impact can be devastating. (Psychologists have observed that one of the most basic human needs, beginning at birth, is to be gazed upon by another. Mothers throughout the world have been observed spending long periods staring into the eyes of their babies with a characteristic tilt of the head. To be seen is to be real, and without another to gaze upon us, we are nothing. Part of the terror of being lost stems from the idea of never being seen again.)

People have known for ages that going from the protection of society into the wild can have a profound effect on the balance of reason and emotion. It can induce altered states of consciousness, hallucinations, even death. The word "bewildered," with its definite, familiar Anglo-Saxon ring, dates from 1684 and comes from the archaic verb, "wilder." To "wilder" someone means to lead him into the woods and get him lost. But a recent Webster's dictionary definition retains much of the original Old English sense:

Bewilder, *v.t.*; bewildered, *pt., pp.*; bewildering, *ppr.* [Dan. *forvilde*, to bewilder; G. *verwildern*; AS. *wilde*, wild.]
1. to confuse hopelessly; befuddle; puzzle.
2. to cause (a person) to be lost in a wilderness. [Archaic.]
Syn.—daze, dazzle, confound, mystify, puzzle, astonish, perplex, confuse, mislead.

Bewilderment, *n.* 1. the fact or state of being bewildered; a chaotic state of mental forces; perplexity.

Wild, *a.* [ME. *wilde, wielde*, from AS. *wild*, wild, bewildered, confused.]

The more modern term "woods shock," which is used by psychologists, dates from at least 1873, where it appeared in the journal *Nature*. It refers to a state of confusion that can beset people in the wilderness.

"'Woods shock' is a term for the fear associated with complete loss of spatial orientation," Kenneth Hill told me. "None of the rational abilities that the victim had before being lost are useful to him anymore." In severe cases, the actions of even the most experienced outdoorsmen can seem inexplicable. Hikers have abandoned full backpacks; hunters have left their guns behind. Killip neglected to make fire or shelter.

But in the light of recent advances in neuroscience, woods shock can now be seen as an emotional survival response associated with the failure of the mental map to match the environment. Thrashing does not save a drowning person either, but it's just as natural. Those who can float quietly have a better chance.

· · ·

Everyone who dies out there dies of confusion. There is always a destructive synergy among numerous factors, including exhaustion, dehydration, hypothermia, anxiety, hunger, injury. So woods shock, which can now be explained in the more precise terms of neuroscience, led Ken Killip to frantic, poorly planned actions. Those stresses and actions incapacitated him even further in a tightening spiral until reason and emotion, instead of working in harmony to produce correct action, became like two drowning swimmers, dragging each other down.

Being lost, then, is not a location; it is a transformation. It is a failure of the mind. It can happen in the woods or it can happen in life. People know that instinctively. A man leaves a perfectly good family for a woman half his age and makes a mess of it, and people say, he got off the path; he lost his way. If he doesn't get back on, he'll lose the self, too. A corporation can do the same thing.

The research suggests five general stages in the process a person goes through when lost. In the first, you deny that you're disoriented and press on with growing urgency, attempting to make your mental map fit what you see. In the next stage, as you realize that you're genuinely lost, the urgency blossoms into a full-scale survival emergency. Clear thought becomes impossible and action becomes frantic, unproductive, even dangerous. In the third stage (usually following injury or exhaustion), you expend the chemicals of emotion and form a strategy for finding some place that matches the mental map. (It is a misguided strategy, for there is no such place now: You are lost.) In the fourth stage, you deteriorate both rationally and emotionally, as the strategy fails to resolve the conflict. In the final stage, as you run out of options and energy, you must become resigned to your plight. Like it or not, you must make a new mental map of where you are. You must become Robinson Crusoe or you will die. To survive, you must find yourself. Then it won't matter where you are.

The stages of getting lost apply to more than just hiking in the woods. A company, such as Xerox, ignores cues from a changing world and from inside its own research facility in Palo Alto and nearly destroys itself. In 1959, Xerox introduced its 914 copier. *Fortune* said it was "the most successful product ever marketed in America." By 1969, Xerox passed $1 billion in sales. In 1971, flushed with success (an emotional state of high arousal), the company's officers were in a stage of deep denial. The world was changing, and they weren't taking in any new information. Their cup was full. At the stockholders' meeting that year, these words, which would nearly destroy the company, were uttered: "We can handle all your information needs." Xerox's leaders had decided to take on IBM, despite all the clear evidence that it would most likely kill them to do so. They were like the snowmobilers, flushed with emotion, who went up that hill, despite the clear evidence that it would probably kill them. They were bending the map, too.

Xerox spent $1 billion to purchase a computer company. At the same time, the company opened the Palo Alto

Research Center (PARC). It took only five years (which is like five days for a hiker) for the computer business to drag Xerox down by about $85 million in cash. In the meantime, scientists and engineers at PARC were inventing the mouse, Ethernet, the graphical user interface, the flat-panel display, and the laser printer. Others got rich off of those inventions. Xerox, busy with its mental models that did not match the real world, saw none of that profit.

Unlike Ken Killip, Xerox is still in the woods.

The stages of getting lost resemble the five stages of dying described by Elisabeth Kübler-Ross, the psychologist who wrote *On Death and Dying*: denial, anger, bargaining, depression, and acceptance. The end result is often the same. "Once the stage of psychological disintegration is reached, death is often not far away," John Leach writes in *Survival Psychology*. "[T]he ability people possess to die gently, and often suddenly, through no organic cause, is a very real one." This suggests that some cases listed as hypothermia may not have been.

That's a lesson Kenneth Hill knows well. "I have photos of a man who settled into a cozy bed of pine needles after removing his shoes, pants, and jacket and setting his wallet on a nearby rock," he told me. "In the photos, he seems so peaceful; it's hard to believe he's dead. The photos have special significance for me, because I helped coordinate the search. Whenever I start to believe I'm some hot-shit SAR expert, I pull the photos out and I'm over it."

Consciousness is a murky, intermittent phenomenon that has yet to be debugged. It sees the world through a glass darkly, not face to face, as Paul the Apostle said. Many conditions influence how you perceive and how much you perceive, as well as what you do with that information. So you go unconsciously about your business, losing your keys and finding them right under your nose. Running red lights. Letting the pot boil over. Forgetting to pay the electric bill. The consequences are few. Then you go into the wilderness, where the consequences are many.

. . .

By his third night lost in the wild, when Killip awoke amid the hailstones at the foot of Terra Tomah Mountain, he had arguably passed through the stages of denial (descending the wrong drainage), panic (climbing up the dangerous scree slope), and strategic planning (attempting to backtrack), and was well into the penultimate stage of deterioration. But he did not succumb to resignation.

That happens in a lot of cases (including big companies, troubled marriages, sick people, lost souls). There are great survivors and helpless victims on the curve of human ability. Most of us are neither. Most of us fall somewhere in between and may perform poorly at first, then find the inner resources to return to correct action and clear thought. If the object of the game is survival, that will do. Or, as my father used to tell me about flying, "A good landing is any landing that you can walk away from."

Killip pulled himself together. He put on his fishing waders and started walking around to get warm. He made a fire and built a makeshift shelter using his garbage bags. (Both were things he should have done the first day, but better late than never.) For the next two days, he stayed put and attended to the business of adapting to the environment, keeping the organism in balance, the process called survival. Killip had entered the final stage that separates the quick from the dead:

not helpless resignation but a pragmatic acceptance of—and even wonder at—the world in which he found himself. He had at last begun to model and map his real environment instead of the one he wished for. He'd worked out his own salvation. He had discovered the first Rule of Life: *Be here now*.

That final stage in the process of being lost can prove to be either a beginning or an end. Some give up and die. Others stop denying and begin surviving. You don't have to be an elite performer. You don't have to be perfect. You just have to get on with it and do the next right thing.

Having faced the reality of his situation, having created a mental map of where he was, not where he wanted to be, Killip was now able to function. On his fifth and final day, he watched as a helicopter passed right over him, so close that "I felt like I could throw a rock at him. Then it turned and flew away. It was almost breaking my spirit."

One of the toughest steps a survivor has to take is to discard the hope of rescue, just as he discards the old world he left behind and accepts the new one. There is no other way for his brain to settle down. Although that idea seems paradoxical, it is essential. I know that's what my father did in the Nazi prison camp: He made it his world. Dougal Robertson, who was cast away at sea for thirty-eight days, advised thinking of it this way: "Rescue will come as a welcome interruption of . . . the survival voyage."

The helicopter pilot had seen Killip's blue parka hanging on a branch and directed the ground searchers to his location. "I lost thirty pounds in five days," Killip told me. His knee injuries required two operations. Today, he still goes into the wilderness, but "now I carry a survival pack and a map and compass everywhere. And I'm very careful about who I go out with. If I have a bad feeling about something, I don't go."

• • •

One of the many baffling mysteries concerns who survives and who doesn't. "It's not what you'd predict, either," Hill, who has studied the survival rates of different demographic groups, told me. "Sometimes the one who survives is an inexperienced female hiker, while the experienced hunter gives up and dies in one night, even when it's not that cold. The category that has one of the highest survival rates is children six and under, the very people we're most concerned about." Despite the fact that small children lose body heat faster than adults, they often survive in the same conditions better than experienced hunters, better than physically fit hikers, better than former members of the military or skilled sailors. And yet one of the groups with the poorest survival rates is children ages seven to twelve. Clearly, those youngest children have a deep secret that trumps knowledge and experience.

Scientists do not know exactly what that secret is, but the answer may lie in basic childhood traits. At that age, the brain has not yet developed certain abilities. For example, small children do not create the same sort of mental maps adults do. They don't understand traveling to a particular place, so they don't run to get somewhere beyond their field of vision. They also follow their instincts. If it gets cold, they crawl into a hollow tree to get warm. If they're tired, they rest, so they don't get fatigued. If they're thirsty, they drink. They try to make themselves comfortable, and staying comfortable helps keep them alive. (Small children following their instincts can also be hard to find; in more than one case, the lost child actually hid from rescuers. One was afraid of "coyotes" when he heard the search dogs barking. Another was afraid of one-eyed monsters when he saw big men wearing headlamps. Fortunately, both were ultimately found.) The secret may also lie in the fact that they do not yet have the sophisticated mental mapping ability that adults have, and so do not try to bend the map. They remap the world they're in.

Children between the ages of seven and twelve, on the other hand, have some adult characteristics, such as mental mapping, but they don't have adult judgment. They don't ordinarily have the strong ability to control emotional responses and to reason through their situation. They panic and run. They look for shortcuts. If a trail peters out, they keep going, ignoring thirst, hunger, and cold, until they fall over. In learning to think more like adults, it seems, they have suppressed the very instincts that might have helped them. But they haven't learned to stay cool. Many may not yet be self-reliant. (One of my survival instructors told me that inner-city children did better in survival training than ones from the suburbs, "because the suburban children have no predators.") They have begun to learn to navigate, to make detailed mental maps; children that age trade secret routes and shortcuts. But a little knowledge is dangerous. A child that age will run across a road without stopping when lost.

We like to think that education and experience make us more competent, more capable. But it seems that the opposite is sometimes true. Ultimately, after years of chasing the ghost of the boy aviator who went on to become my father, I went to survival school to try to find out if there was a way to learn the skills of survival while retaining the instincts of a small child. I thought that perhaps through all the risk taking, the quest for cool, I had wandered off the path of life. I couldn't help thinking, then, of the Zen concept of the beginner's mind, the mind that remains open and ready despite years of training. "In the beginner's mind there are many possibilities," said Zen master Shunryu Suzuki. "In the expert's mind there are few."

WHITE SHARK
ARCHIBALD RUTLEDGE

Although Archibald Rutledge (1883–1973) was best known for his hunting stories in outdoor magazines, collected in many books such as The American Hunter, *he was a prolific poet (the first Poet Laureate of South Carolina), author of spiritual books, and a keen naturalist. He wrote more than fifty books and poems while teaching at Mercersburg Academy in Pennsylvania and also maintained his family plantation, Hampton, on the banks of the Santee River in South Carolina. Among the fine tales from Rutledge's experiences with nature, "White Shark" stands out as one that researchers of shark attacks might give further study. There are two narrow escapes from sharks in the tale, and the second is clearly connected to a 1916 incident at the Jersey Shore in which Rutledge and his family encountered a shark that killed one man before Rutledge's eyes and then swam up Matteawan River and killed two more people and injured another. Like many others, Rutledge believed the attacks were by a great white shark, but most of today's experts who have studied the subject believe a bull shark was to blame. Whether you are interested in this story because of the sensational 1916 attacks or just looking for a good read, Archibald Rutledge won't let you down.*

. . .

While still a teacher in Pennsylvania, I had what seemed to me a very uncomfortably close call with a great white shark, which is justly called "the terror of the deep." As I have said before, my whole long life has been rather adventurous; but no experience in my memory contained so many dangerous possibilities. Some of these adventures include being dragged for an unfortunate distance by a mean-tempered horse; being kicked in the head by a horse; being struck by a deadly cottonmouth moccasin—also by an aggressive diamondback rattlesnake; charged by a wild cow in the woods, when I inadvertently walked too close to her baby calf, which she had hidden away in the tall grass; caught by a big shark at night, all alone; having a running battle with a monstrous wild boar, an old brigand of the swamps, which did his best to get his tusks into me; and having assorted encounters with sundry grim bull alligators. But my meeting with the white shark was to me the most memorable of all.

When a man tells of one of his adventures, it is easy to accuse him of bragging. Many a good story has been lost through fear of just such an accusation. Yet wild escapades do happen. They are true; and I think they should be recorded without having the teller of the tale charged with inflating himself. This white shark business distinctly does not make me a hero. Nor does anything else. Yet, whatever my life has lacked in serious accomplishment, my days on this earth have at least been *lively* ones.

Before recounting this particular experience, I think it well to say something about sharks in general; for people are taking far more interest than ever in the shark as a possible, or likely, killer.

Although the weird-looking hammerhead, or, in my long experience, *any* large shark, can be dangerous, only the great white shark is the true man-eater. The bathing beaches of South Africa, and those of Australia and New Zealand, are regularly equipped with heavy wire shark-nets. Although usually an inhabitant of tropical waters, when the northward surge of springtime begins, some of these great creatures, together with many other "displaced persons" of the Deep, will move northward. Though rarely, white sharks have been caught off the coast of New England; as late as 1962 one of these dangerous brutes, twenty-six feet long, was caught off the Atlantic coast. This real terror of the ocean, in modern times, grows to an extreme length of forty feet; but it is fortunate for us that we were not surf-bathers in an earlier age of the earth's long history. Judging by the fossil teeth found in beds of phosphate and marl, in sand-pits, and in such tall sand cliffs as overlook the Chesapeake Bay below Annapolis, the ancient white shark grew to a length of ninety feet. It is difficult for us to imagine such a monster. But he was here. His passing is unlamented. The scientists call the white shark *Carcharodon*.

The only shark known to inhabit fresh water is the very dangerous one found in Lake Nicaragua. Although rarely more than eight feet in length, this shark is peculiarly savage and aggressive. However, it has long been my observation that sharks do not hesitate to penetrate coastal rivers. I have seen a large one in a river eight miles from the ocean. Curiously, he seemed to be investigating the possibilities of dining on a big alligator; and that scaly dragon eyed the shark appraisingly.

It has always seemed to me an almost providential thing that any shark usually (but not always) betrays his presence by his tall dorsal fin. Sharks travel in water at many depths, and come to the surface only when attracted by something. However, they should be classed as surface fishes.

When fishing by day with a hand-line in the creeks and bays, I always had a shark-line out, using a demijohn as a float. Without a float, a big shark's initial stroke was liable to upset my small light boat. I caught scores of sharks of many kinds and sizes: The sand, the tiger, the nurse, the leopard, the hammerhead, and one white shark. The largest I ever took on a line was a leopard shark that measured twelve feet, ten inches. Believe me, that is plenty of shark!

While fishing, I could usually tell when a shark was near. The spots, the whiting and trout, the yellowtail and the cor-valli that had kept me so busy (I remember that on one flood tide I caught ninety-six nice fish that I could sell), would suddenly stop biting. This made me almost sure that a shark had come up. I would then begin to watch my demijohn, and usually it would disappear in a fountain of foam. This would mean that I had a shark, and must take care of him.

To do this, I usually pulled up the anchor, rowed to the shore, and hauled the shark up high and dry. Year after year I fished in this way, incidentally learning a good deal about sharks. But my real hassle came at night; when I used to set a gill-net, chiefly for mullets. With one of the nets, with the incoming tide about half high, I stopped off the mouth of a small creek. There was phosphorus in the creek, and I could see plenty of fish in the water. Taking an oar, I would walk up the side of the creek, whacking the water with the flat of the oar to run the fish back into the net. There was no light but starlight. As I could see many fish darting back toward the net, I turned back that way myself. As I neared the net, I could see the water boiling, and the corks on the net being violently jerked down. To reach the netted fish I got down in the warm water, which was about breast-high. Soon I was tossing fish over the net into my boat on the other side. I was about halfway across the creek when suddenly a warm wave rose almost to my neck. Then the huge hulk of something rasped by one of my legs. I realized that my trouser-leg had been literally rubbed off. At the same time my leg began to smart and burn furiously. I knew it must be a shark, with that sandpaper hide of his. I realized, too, that there must be some blood in the water. Under those conditions, a shark can be at his worst. The smell of blood always sets one of these permanently ravenous creatures crazy. Catching the net with my right hand, and extending my left, I headed for the shore. As the bottom of the creek was muddy, my progress was slow. I was in a spot, and I knew it. But I did not anticipate what happened next. The shark was swimming for me, and his mouth was wide open. What designs he had on me—if any—I shall never know. But I would not attribute any sensitiveness or sympathy to such a brute. The next thing I knew, my left hand was deep in the open mouth of the shark, and I felt the cutting edges of the serrated teeth. I tried gently to withdraw my hand, but I felt his jaws closing, and he rose, as if following my hand *to me*. I pulled my left hand away, turned the net loose, and as I made out his monstrous head almost clear of the water, I drove both fists into his face, yelled at him, and made a dash for the bank. I got up safely, and lay down on a pile of sedge. Looking at my net, I saw it buckle as the shark tore through the idle of it; then I saw his fearsome bulk outlined in the phosphorescent water. In starlight, any observation I could make was, I knew, conjectural; but I had a pretty good knowledge of sharks, and I judged this one to be close to fifteen feet.

A round hole had been rasped away from my right trouser leg, and the skin was rather badly torn. I had forgotten about my hand until I felt the blood running down all over it. Although that was more than fifty years ago, I bear to this day the scars of that encounter. My left hand was pretty badly cut up.

Always when I got home, at any time of night, I would stretch my net between two trees to dry. The next morning when I looked at it, there was a hole through it fully three feet in diameter.

I often think of that night; of the dim sea-marsh stretching away on every side, of the sound of fish breaking water; of the starlight, which enabled me to see pretty well after I got used to it. And I think of that monster of the deep that really had me at his mercy. More and more I consider my escape a miraculous one.

Strange to say, two of the very largest sharks—the whale shark and the basking shark—are harmless to man. However, although they have no record as man-eaters, I believe a safe rule to follow in regard to any wild creature of the land or water is this: If it *can* hurt you, be careful—always remembering that these children of Nature have not read the books that say they will not harm a human being. And even when a species is known to be usually harmless, you never know when you may encounter a rogue, a mother with her young, or a creature smouldering with rage because of a festering wound. Even so famous a scientist as William Bebee has gone on record as saying that a shark will never hurt a human being. Well, I have a friend who lost the whole calf of his left leg to a shark; and I have seen the bodies of four men when sharks got through with them. I actually saw a man killed in the surf of a New Jersey beach. What my own eyes saw was far more persuasive than Mr. Bebee's opinion. A shark can mangle a human body almost beyond recognition. It is a devilish mutilation.

Despite many views to the contrary, a shark never has to turn over in order to seize his prey.

I used to take my wife and three small sons to one of the New Jersey beaches for a vacation. We were at different times at Atlantic City, Beach Haven, and Cape May. As I do not care to give any summer resort a bad name, I shall not mention the exact location of the scene of this adventure of mine, but to this day it remains one of the most popular of summer resorts, famous especially for its fine fishing.

Late one August afternoon we drove up to the hotel where we were to stay. As the weather was cloudy and cool, my wife decided to stay in our room, while my boys and I dressed for swimming and strolled down on the beach. There was a rather mean offshore wind blowing. As it was gusty and chill, we decided to stay out of the water. There were practically no people on the beach. But our attention was attracted to a young man standing in the breakers, with the water about up to his waist. Even as we watched him, admiring the beauty of his build, he suddenly threw both hands high over his head, at the same time giving a terrible cry. In a moment he had crumpled down in the shallow surf. I could see the water reddening where he had stood; and in a moment I saw something else that completed the sinister nature of the picture. I saw only the tip of a white dorsal fin, and I knew we had seen a young man killed by a shark.

Later, a part of the body was recovered, cruelly mangled I was told. I learned also that the unfortunate bather had been a young lawyer, the son of a prominent Philadelphia family.

Of course, as soon as this tragedy occurred, a great crowd quickly gathered. As I had apparently been closer to the victim than any one else when the fatal attack occurred, I was interviewed by several officials, one of whom was incredulous that I could identify the killer.

As soon as the ambulance left, the crowd quickly dispersed, casting misgiving eyes at the roiling waters. Some of them were probably wondering, as I was, if this was a good place to spend a vacation.

As my little boys and I walked on, the beach became bare again—except for a rather buxom mother and her little daughter, about five years old. I do not believe they knew what had happened behind them.

The child had a rather large toy balloon, and this she kept tossing up and catching. I knew it would be only a matter of time before a gusty flaw would carry the balloon into the surf, under which the ebbtide was pacing out with fearful urgency. I was about to run forward to warn the mother not to let her daughter go into the surf, when a sudden gust carried the balloon some twenty feet out in the water. The child splashed after it, uttering little cries of dismay. Of course, the mother rushed after the child.

I looked wildly around for help. I might save one, but not both. I could not see a soul near, not even a lifeguard. By this time the mother and child were almost one hundreds yards offshore. I could swim, but was not a strong swimmer. However, I felt that this was a situation that clamored for my help. Telling my wide-eyed boys not to leave the beach, I ran into the water and struck out for the people I hoped, in some way, to rescue. I did not have much faith in the success of my mission, but at least I could try.

Neither the mother nor her little daughter seemed to be swimming. They were just floating and tossing on top of the water. The ebb was relentlessly taking them seaward about as fast as I could swim. While I was riding high in the surf, there came another development, and a sinister one at that. Just outside the line of breakers the water was not very rough; and now cutting through it was that evil fin, the sign and symbol of prowling death. It must be the same shark! Had he located the helpless mother and child? Now and then the fin would be submerged; and I did not know at what moment it might rise under us or close beside one of us three. Deciding that if I rescued any one, my best chance would be with the child, I turned toward her, swimming as fast as I could.

Suddenly a lithe and powerful form shot by me, going like a guided missile. I gasped, thinking it was the shark! But it was a life-guard. But, to my dismay, he sped toward the child, leaving the rather hefty mother to me. I accepted the challenge and swam toward the lady. Once I saw the fin of the huge shark only about twenty feet beyond her. When I reached her, to my immense relief, I found her helpful and by no means hysterical. She had a bright red scarf tied about her head; and I had no way of knowing whether this would attract or repel the circling killer.

I asked her to turn over on her back, which she did swiftly. She seemed quite buoyant. Certainly she had not been dieting.

Getting my left arm around her, and on my back myself, I began with one arm, the toilsome swim back toward the beach.

When I told her that her little girl was safe, I saw tears running down one side of her face. She began talking to me.

"Young man," she said, to my surprise, "did you see that shark? Do you think we can make it to the beach?"

Although I was dubious, I assured her that we could. Glancing toward the beach, I saw that it was black with people; and I caught a glimpse of the guard as he carried the rescued child ashore in his arms. I told the mother.

"Thank God," she breathed. "But my husband will never forgive me for this escapade."

She then began to paddle with her hands and to kick with her feet to help us along. My swimming became automatic, and I was conscious of great weariness.

"Can you swim at all?" I asked. "If so, we are close enough now for you to make it to shore. I'll get there, too, somehow."

"I hope you don't think I'd leave you?" she asked.

I felt that the way we were going then both of us might be drowned. Yet she was saying she would not leave me—a fine true feminine role. If I was to drown, she would go with me. For some reason this resolve of hers gave me renewed strength; and only a little later the golden moment came when my feet touched the blessed sands near the shore.

All this time no help had been offered us; but as soon as we reached shore, we were encumbered with help.

I saw the little girl safe in her dear mother's arms. My own boys were waiting for me; and it was good to feel their hands in mine as we walked back to the hotel.

"Dad, we watched you when you brought her in," said my eldest.

"Didn't you see the shark?" asked the next oldest.

"You swimmed a good swam," said my baby. That was reward enough for my effort.

But that night the lady's husband called on me to thank me. He was from Pittsburgh, and said he could easily get me a Carnegie Medal. I refused to be decorated, and have ever since regretted my foolish decision. My wife was amazed to hear of my adventure, for I had told her nothing, and had asked my boys to be quiet about the whole affair. I think it makes a woman nervous if she knows that her husband will risk his life to save another woman.

This story has a sequel. On the flood tide the next morning that shark (it *must* have been the same one) went up the Matteawan River, which winds through the New Jersey marshes. Of three boys swimming there, this massive brute killed two of them, and badly mangled the third. By that time men began to drop heavy wire nets before and behind the shark. Then came the local hunters with their highpowered rifles. There was not enough water in the tidewater stream to hide this monster. The hunters shot and killed him. When he was hauled ashore he proved to be a true white shark, eighteen feet and ten inches in length—plenty of man-eater, at any time, anywhere.

A PLAN TO RECOVER THE TRAIL

CARY J. GRIFFITH

Because it is one of my favorite canoe-trip destinations, the Boundary Waters Canoe Area on the Minnesota-Ontario border brings my attention to full alert when it is mentioned. Both the BWCA and the adjoining Canadian Quetico Provincial Park are true wilderness areas with massive forests and countless lakes. Outboard motors and float planes are not allowed, making these destinations two of today's greatest wilderness experiences for canoe trips, camping, and fishing. I've had so much fun in my own ventures into this great region that it's hard to imagine that such trips can turn into a survival experience. Yet, I know it happens. The wrong turn, the wrong trail ... Cary Griffith's wonderful book, Lost in the Wild, *tells two stories of near tragedy. This excerpt shows how close Jason Rasmussen got to the brink before rescuers finally arrived.*

■ ■ ■

NORTHEAST OF THE POW WOW TRAIL, WEDNESDAY, OCTOBER 24, 2001

In the morning Jason awakens to a light rain pattering on his tent fly. He opens his eyes to the gray light, comfortable and warm in his mummy bag. Then he rolls over, closes his eyes and listens. The drops make small pelting sounds directly overhead. He feels as though he is completely alone in the universe. The immediacy of having a paper-thin layer of nylon between himself and wild woods makes him feel alive.

He feels a satisfying ache that leads him to quickly recall yesterday's trek. As he comes more fully awake he remembers his long peregrination through the woods. He can feel the dull muscle ache from yesterday's heavy hauling through wet brush. It is the kind of stiffness that reminds him of the value of hard exercise. But he doesn't want to feel that level of discomfort again—wet, cold, and bone-tired.

Warm and dry in his mummy bag, he is not thinking about being lost and is certainly not awaiting rescue. He has plenty of water, food, and shelter. If he is careful with his supplies, he could last two weeks, though it would never come to that. With a fire, and the bright tent on the treeless escarpment, a plane could easily find him. It would be over in a day.

But he is not yet ready to concede being entirely lost, and after all, it is only Wednesday. He is still disappointed with himself over carelessly losing his Fisher map, but he knows he has plenty of time to find his own way out. This morning—rested, warm, and dry—he feels more optimistic than he did yesterday, after a long day wandering through wilderness. The rain outside keeps him tent-bound, but he is happy in his comfortable surroundings. And he will use the time to figure out his whereabouts and make a plan.

He squirms out of the bag, opens the tent flap, and stretches in the light, cold rain. He steps a few paces across the bed of caribou moss. Walking on the moss-covered wet rock is like stepping onto an icy sponge. He looks down over the long, narrow lake in front of him. It is surrounded by the usual thick tree line, the occasional low-hung cedar bent out over its surface. Under the muted sky the lake is slate gray. It appears to stretch more than a quarter mile south. There is mist at the far end of the lake and it looks beautiful in the early morning rain.

But it's cold outside, and he climbs back in out of the rain and slips into his mummy bag. He pulls the opening up to his neck and waits until his body warms the bag. Then he reaches out, rummages through his pack for a granola bar, and happily munches, washing down the breakfast snack with lake water.

He pulls out the *Hiking Minnesota* map and studies it. There isn't a lot of detail. He examines the lakes on the simple depiction. He is looking for something resembling the lake in front of his tent. He stares at the map for a couple of minutes.

His first night he thinks he camped near Pose Lake. According to the map he should have been close to it. Even though he made more turns than an interstate cloverleaf, he suspects he ended up somewhere in the middle of the circular trail. That is, somewhere inside the twenty-six-mile-long oval that marks the trail's boundaries.

He considers the lake in front of him, long and without islands. As he stares at the map he sees an obvious choice, a thin gray strip inside the Pow Wow circumference. Fallen Arch Lake stretches near the eastern end of the oval, its southern end reaching down almost to the bottom of the trail. If he is correct—if the lake in front of him is Fallen Arch—Jason realizes he may be closer than he thinks to getting out of here. If he walks along the western side of the lake and strikes off beyond its southern shores, at some point he will cross the Pow Wow. He examines the map, looks at the key, and uses a brief length of finger to determine the distance from the bottom of the lake to the trail. It looks close, less than a mile from the southern tip.

He opens the tent flap and looks out over Fallen Arch Lake. Some of its shoreline doesn't exactly align with what he sees on the map. But the map's depiction is so simple and without detail, there is no way to be certain. They are both long and narrow, they are both north–south. When he examines the simple map, the only gray swatch that even remotely compares to it is Fallen Arch. It has to be Fallen Arch.

The rain is still pattering his tent. From inside his pack he extracts the pamphlet he purchased at REI, Suzanne Swedo's *Wilderness Survival: Staying Alive Until Help Arrives*. He's not going anywhere in this rain. He hungers for something to read, and apart from the map and a copy of some of the pages from the Pukite text, this is it.

He begins at the beginning. The pamphlet is small, and he is a good student. Within an hour he has skimmed the entire booklet.

It's a clear, well-reasoned approach to surviving in the wild. The author is emphatic about the three most important requirements of staying alive: shelter, water, and food. She explains their relative importance, given climate and terrain. In the North Woods, Jason realizes, water is abundant. No problem there. But in October in these woods, shelter rises in importance. The human body, he reads, can survive a long time without food, as long as it is well hydrated and reasonably warm. Reading about starvation makes him hungry, and he rummages his pack for another granola bar.

As Jason reads through the text, he notes he has all three covered. He could live like this for over a week. Longer, truth be told. He reads about some of the forest's edibles—which don't really sound that edible. Cattails, conifers, and grasses. The inner bark of some trees. Earthworms and grubs. He is amazed by the forest flora and fauna that can sustain life. The text says very little about flavor, and he doesn't recall seeing pine bark, cattail roots, or raw larvae on any restaurant menus, but if you need to stay alive there are at least a few wild comestibles offering nourishment.

When he is finished it is still raining. He reads through the text a second time. Water, shelter, food—in that order. He is well positioned for a long stay in the wilderness, though he knows it will never come to that.

He peruses the text a third time, absently opening it to chapter six: "Shelter From Cold and Heat." He reads the first paragraph.

Should you become involved in a wilderness emergency, you are statistically much more likely to succumb to hypothermia, otherwise known as exposure, than to any other problem. If you can stay warm enough to make it through the first night, you're probably going to make it to safety or at least survive long enough to be rescued.

He reads about "the recipe for hypothermia: cold, wetness, and wind." He considers freezing from a clinical perspective. In the last five years he has learned plenty about the body's operation. But this discussion of hypothermia from a wilderness-survival perspective is new. When they covered it in medical school, it was brief and cursory. Today, in his tent, the notion has an immediacy difficult to ignore. *People in the northern climes*, he thinks, *are always close to the possibility.*

He dog-ears the page on hypothermia and lays the book down. He leans back to consider the world's northern climates. He loses himself in contemplation, wondering about it. And then he notices the pattering has stopped. There is only the sound of water forming large drops near his tent's ridgeline, rolling down its sides.

Jason returns to his pack and gets into the warm clothes he'll need to hike through the woods. While he dresses, he decides it will be much easier hiking through dense brush without the encumbrance of his backpack. He recalls yesterday's struggle through tree branches and fallen boughs.

His jacket has more than enough pockets, and he has brought along a fanny pack with two water bottle slots. Now he rummages his pack for some of the items he'll need for his short hike south to find the trail: a couple of small packages of crackers, a can of tuna, two Tootsie Rolls, a package of cocoa, his compass, a Swiss Army knife. He considers the items randomly, trying to figure out the minimum required to hike through the woods for probably less than two miles. All he needs are sufficient supplies to get him south of the lake point and less than a mile into the trees. He should be able to discover the trail's whereabouts and identify the easiest path to get there. He can focus on finding the southern loop, and on marking the best trail for returning to it when he recovers his supplies.

He places two water bottles in the slots on either side of his waist pack and picks it up, weighing it. Not bad, he thinks. *Much easier getting through these woods without that damn pack*, he thinks.

By noon the skies have been quiet for almost an hour. The world is wet and overcast, cold, but not freezing. Jason laces his boots, puts on his olive drab jack with the internal hood, fastens his pockets, and zips up the coat. He decides against taking a pair of gloves and a hat. It is above freezing, and he is trying to be careful about packing light. He doesn't want his jacket bulging and catching on the brush, and he doesn't want unnecessary weight hampering his progress.

Finally, he feels ready. He fastens the fanny pack around his waist and steps out of his tent, bending back to zip up the fly and close the opening.

He carries his disposable camera out of the tent. He starts down the hillock toward the western edge of the lake. After ten paces he turns and takes another picture of his tent. The rise looks dull, gray, and wet, with a small backdrop of spruce. He knows it would be hard to find by dead reckoning, but he has an entire lake to assist him. When he returns, all he needs to do is find the lake. Find the lake, he reasons, and he can easily recover his tent.

He turns and in the midday gray descends the granite rise. After being cooped up in the tent through the morning he feels good to be walking. Within five minutes he is in trees so dense—cedar and low-hung black spruce—that he cannot even see his tent or the granite rise behind him. But he is careful to keep the lake on his left.

Walking this close to water, he finds that parts of the shoreline are heavily bouldered. Fallen branches form an obstacle course. Whenever necessary, Jason climbs over, ducks under, or walks around large toppled trees. His progress is slow, but he is happy to be hiking again, particularly without his pack. Hiking through thick wood with his pack isn't going to be easy. Periodically he reminds himself to look for the best route. But for the most part he moves down the shoreline toward the end of the lake on automatic pilot, attending to the next ten yards, the part in front of him he can see. He is careful to keep the surface water in sight. As he walks, he ruminates. Wander a tenth of a mile in any direction, and unless you are consciously attending to your thoughts, they can stray far from your immediate trail.

After half an hour Jason comes to the southern lake tip. He peers into the woods. The land's surface makes a gradual rise through the trees. That's good. He wants to stay on higher elevations, no matter how slight. He does not want to encounter another bog. These woods are thick and shadowy, but as they rise away from the lake they appear to open. It looks easier walking just up ahead, and Jason moves toward the space, plotting his next twenty yards.

Well into the trees he turns and can no longer see the lakeshore. He pauses long enough to fish is compass out of his waist pack. He takes a reading and notes the direction due south. He looks ahead and finds a landmark—a huge fallen white pine—that is almost exactly due south. Its path lies a few degrees to the west, but not much. Jason makes for the tree, bending, weaving through the brush.

He was correct about this part of the woods; they are easier to traverse. Here it appears to be old-growth forest with the high tree canopies blocking enough sunlight to minimize the understory growth. He appreciates the change in elevation and more spacious woods. He keeps walking south.

There appears to be a meandering height of land that jogs south-southeast, then south-southwest. If he stays on it, the walking is much more comfortable. Periodically he pulls the compass out of his pocket and takes a reading. The higher jag of land moves in a minimal slant southwards, and it is easy walking in the midday. The forest growth, with towering red firs and occasional white pines, is haunting and beautiful, like walking through a cathedral.

But in places understory growth is still plentiful enough that his pant legs remain damp. Hiking beside the lake, pushing through the dense weave near water's edge, Jason can't help getting wet. But he is dressed for it and comfortable, and the exercise warms him.

He keeps moving vaguely south, admiring the forest. After an hour he is well south of the lake, pushing through another high patch of trees. He hasn't seen anything resembling a trail. Not even a deer trail. Jason wonders if these woods—these woods he is now hiking through—have ever seen the print of man. He tries to imagine what it must have been like to live here, to survive like the indigenous Ojibwe. And while it summons pictures out of books and the cinema—*Dances With Wolves* occurs to him—he knows that their life of hunting and gathering is well beyond his powers of invention.

Nothing in his life—his childhood, his years in med school—was anything like what indigenous people had experienced here before whites arrived. And it wasn't that long ago. One hundred years before, on this very spot, he would have worried about wolves, bears, cougars, and staying alive by whatever he could hunt or hack out of the woods. One hundred years, he reflects, would have been 1901.

He revises his estimate to two hundred years. Two hundred years would have put the date at 1801, a time of traders and voyageurs. At that time, he thinks, trying to recall his early American frontier history, it would have been the Hudson Bay Company and the Northwest Company. He vaguely remembers reading about it as a kid—how the two fur companies fought over this fecund landscape. Fought over beaver to make hats in England, battled over all the fur-bearing animals to make stylish coats and fur-lined gloves. He smiles to remember how the absurd fashions of the time compelled the exploration of a far-off wilderness, and then the death of so many animals thousands of miles away. He has seen enough MTV and cinema—not to mention sitcoms—to know that changing tastes can dictate some bizarre perspectives, if not lives.

He looks up through the trees and realizes he has been walking for the last fifteen minutes without much of a sense of his own direction. He pulls out the compass, examines the needles, and sees his current course is more east than west. And he still hasn't discovered the trail. He has tried to hike where the walking is easiest, staying on higher ground, though in places there wasn't much difference. He has skirted fallen trees and rocky outcrops, but he hasn't even come across a game path, let alone a hiking trail.

He pauses in a cathedral of red and white pine. The walking here is beautiful and relatively open. He could keep moving in a southerly direction—at least for the next fifty yards. Beyond that distance it is difficult to see anything. He reasons that if he hasn't yet discovered the path, maybe he hasn't moved far enough south. He would have guessed his hiking this long would take him at least a mile, but it is hard to determine in the woods. And truth is, he hadn't paid that much attention to the exact time of his departure. He looks down at his wristwatch. It's 1:30. The sky is gray, but there is still plenty of light. He has at least another four or five hours of daylight, and he's still hoping he will discover the trail.

Until now Jason has felt confident about his plan. He'd found the lake on the map and could see the trail just beyond it. Hiking down to the trail was the obvious choice, but he wonders where it is. He may have crossed it, but if so, it is virtually invisible. Now he wonders. He recollects the map, but cannot remember any of the other lakes in the area even partially resembling the lake in front of his tent. It has to be Fallen Arch, which would place him very near the bottom section of trail.

He wonders if he has truly moved in a southerly direction. He takes out the compass and balances it to take another reading. If he continues, he will be moving south-southeast. He wonders if he should try veering west. He looks in that direction, and the forest makes a gentle descent for the next fifty yards. He can't see anything except tree trunks. But the hiking appears to be as easy as it is here.

Maybe if he moves in a westerly direction he will encounter the trail. Maybe he just hasn't gone far enough. And so he decides. He moves in a south-southwest direction. He picks his way carefully through the woods. He wanders as he walks, skirting fallen trees and wet brush. Occasionally he takes a compass reading, but not often. Barring yesterday's anomaly, Jason believes he has a pretty good sense of direction, of dead reckoning, even in woods as dense as these.

He hikes for another half hour, but does not find the path. He decides to try something radical, and hikes due east. Perhaps part of the trail moves in a north–south direction. He tries to remember and thinks the southern end of the trail had plenty of wobble. He guesses it would likely traverse high ground, rather than wet low patches. He stays on the high ground, moving for another fifteen minutes before finally stopping.

When he finally realizes he is not going to find the trail, it is another difficult moment. He cannot believe it. He remembers the map, the way Fallen Arch was so close to the trail. Can the DNR have been that obtuse about marking the Pow Wow Trail? He recalls reading something about signs being prohibited in the BWCAW, something about pure wilderness. *But Christ*, he thinks, *what if the trail's not marked at all?* He thought it would have been traveled enough to at the very least be a visible path. Much of the trail he started on was clear, and wide enough for an ATV. Where is the blasted trail now?

He looks at his watch: 2:30. He guesses he has been walking for at least two hours. Although he has been walking back and forth, he figures if he hikes due north he can make camp in less than an hour. His journey south, east, and west has been so halting and hacked up, he knows if he is determined he can make it back to the lake and then his camp in *less* than an hour. And he is starting to get hungry. He reaches down and pulls one of is water bottles out of his waist pack. A long draught quenches his thirst. He feels for one of the Tootsie Rolls, unwraps it, pops it into his mouth, savors it. He chews slowly, takes another drink, swishing the water to fill his mouth with the dark, chocolaty flavor.

That was good, he thinks. He reaches in for the other roll, eats it with the same relish, knowing he can replenish his supply when he returns to camp.

The water and the Tootsie Rolls temporarily sate his appetite, at least enough to hold him until he gets back to his tent. He hasn't decided what he's going to prepare for supper, but he still has enough hunger to spend a few moments contemplating the possibilities. Another stroganoff? This time maybe his turkey teriyaki? *Whoa*, he thinks. *I've got to get back.*

He fishes out his compass, takes another reading, and strikes off through the trees.

■ ■ ■

After hiking north for more than an hour Jason looks at his watch, looks at the woods in front of him, at the climb of bush and trees spreading away from him. It all appears new, as though it is totally virgin territory.

He fishes out the compass, takes another reading. Yes, he is hiking north. He scours the landscape for a familiar tree, outcropping of rocks, tracks through the leaves. There is nothing.

He keeps walking, and after what he presumes is at least another half-hour he feels something stronger than worry. A first clear wave of panic flows over him. He had been worried when he stopped and took another bearing. Now, not only is he not finding his camp, but the lake itself seems to have disappeared. How could he have lost a lake?

There is still plenty of light, he reasons, trying to calm himself. *There is still time*. He doesn't want to contemplate alternatives. He puts aside other possibilities and keeps walking.

After another hour he can no longer deny he is lost. He can no longer keep walking and expect to encounter the lake, or his gear. But it has to be around here! He hasn't wandered that far. By Jason's recollection it has been a brief two hours, maybe two and a half. And for more than half that time he was heading north, *closer* to his camp. At least he was supposed to be returning.

But where is the lake? Where is Fallen Arch and the beautiful escarpment with the orange tent perched atop it? Where is he? He doesn't want to think about consequences, but as the light continues bleeding from the afternoon sky— already an opaque gray—another wave of panic washes over him. This one threatens to engulf him.

He keeps walking. He pushes through brush and trees for another half-hour. Another wave of panic threatens him, rises inside and crashes along some inner shore, leaving him desolate and mute. And then he sees the opening ahead in the trees.

It has to be the lake! He scrambles toward the opening, elated. He cannot believe he's been that stupid—stupid enough to miss an entire lake. But now he has recovered it. Now he can use the last hour and a half of dull gray light to move up Fallen Arch's shoreline and recover his camp.

And then he pushes through the trees and sees—another bog. Another damn bog? He peers to the west, turns and stares into the gray eastern light. He squints across the bog's surface.

If there is a landscape of the soul, its lowest point must be a bog. Jason struggles to get a grip on himself. He can feel some part of him getting sucked into shadowy desolation. For now, the mottled and tangled surface of the bog—knowing he must cross it—is the single tangible expectation keeping his panic at bay. For now, crossing the bog occupies an imagination that might otherwise drown in the full realization of his predicament.

He turns into the brush, finds a dead tamarack bough, and trims it down to a sturdy five-foot pole. He starts picking his way across the tangled bog's surface. And he makes excellent progress. He is almost to the other side when his last leaping step breaks the bog's surface, starts sucking him down, and he lunges for the far edge. He topples onto firm ground, but his feet and legs are cold and soaked to the upper calf. He watches the black water runnel off his legs and boots. The feeling of cold is far off, and he sits and stares into the tangled surface of the bog, unbelieving, the panic now full in his throat, disarming, forcing him mute and still.

■　■　■

Jason doesn't know how long he has been sitting. Profound panic has given way to catatonia. He cannot move, cannot think. He is trying to figure out how he got here. He is trying to understand it, his legs soaked with water and his boots full of it. The bog has reached up and taken his spirit and he hunches on the edge of it, wanting the sick feeling to be over, wanting to awaken from this nightmare.

Where was the lake? What happened to that lake? The question rises and words form, but there is nothing behind them. He feels outside himself, or in some other landscape. It's starting to occur to him. Gradually, like a far-off wave coming in to curl and crash, his awful predicament is starting to rise over him.

He is wet, cold, tired, and there is not much more than an hour of light left, possibly less. It is the waning light that strikes him, slaps him at least partially awake. If he has to stay in these woods for the entire night, with the temperature dropping fast, the smell of storm in the air, he might not see tomorrow's dawn.

The thought of dying makes him rise. He has no idea where to turn, where to find shelter. He looks across the bog but knows a return south is out of the question. He has to push north. He climbs through the boggy shoreline into the trees. He is looking for something, he doesn't know what. He is searching through dusk for some place to hide—some place to pack himself away for the evening where he can roll up in a fetal ball, conserve his heat, and survive.

He stumbles through the woods like a somnambulist. He is devastated. He is trying to remove himself, trying to bring himself awake, but he's beyond conscious thought. He is tired, and he tries to focus on his mission—to find someplace to hide, someplace to sleep, someplace safe, out of the weather, out of the cold.

But he *is* cold. He can feel it as he walks. His legs are still wet and stiff and his feet are numb. His brain isn't functioning. It is as though the freezing water has reached around his cerebral cortex and deadened it with an icy grip.

Up ahead he comes to a boulder as large as a house. He walks around the base and sees a very small depression. He gets down on his hands and knees, looks at it abstractedly. He might be able to dig it out. He pulls some small boulders out of the space, but then looks at it and realizes it would be more work than he has time to burrow. And besides, the rocks are cold. The entire landscape is freezing.

He walks away from the boulder. He wanders another five minutes through the woods, absent and searching. He doesn't know what to think. He doesn't know what to look for. He is dimly aware this may be his last walk anywhere. He tries to put it out of his mind, to keep moving through the woods.

Up ahead he sees a huge, fallen pine. It's in a forest of giant trees. The woods are dark and forbidding. The tree is fallen on its side, at a slant where it snapped off a few feet up its trunk.

He walks up to the toppled tree. It has been lying here awhile. He considers building a lean-to. He looks around the woods for material, but there are only thin boughs and dead wood. These would afford no protection from the wind. And he didn't pack matches. He has no means to build a fire. *I didn't pack matches.* He repeats it to himself, but he is a long ways from registering its full impact. He is numb.

The air is turning colder, and he thinks he smells snow.

He looks at the fallen tree, at the dusky woods around

him. It feels hopeless. *Maybe somewhere else*, he thinks. *Maybe if I keep moving?* He turns and walks another fifty yards. When he comes to the end of it, he is in the same woods he has been in for most of the day. There is still a half-hour of light, but it is rapidly getting dark.

He stands and tries to think. He suspects he has seen something he could use to make a shelter, somewhere in the latest ground he's covered. It is one of his first truly coherent thoughts since panic first set in. He tries to recall the land-scape. The boulder. The tree.

He could keep moving forward, searching through the woods until they darken. But he knows there's not much time. He needs to use whatever he's seen in the last twenty min-utes. There is no time to keep searching. He turns and starts retracing his steps. Fifty yards later he is back at the tree.

The boulder would take too long to burrow out. It would be well after dark before he could fashion a cave big enough. And then what about the cave's mouth? Cold seeks the lowest elevation. The cold would sweep into the gap and freeze him into a fetal fist. He stands beside the fallen tree, reconsidering his idea of building a lean-to. He tries to recall something from his book on wilderness survival. He can't remember anything. He can't figure out how he could make a lean-to with enough cover to retain his body heat. Its sides would be a sieve, and the wind would sough through it all evening. He'd be dead by morning, or near dead. He reaches up and absently breaks away part of the end of the huge fallen tree. It is rotted. Its center is heavy with decay.

He tries to focus. Something he has seen over the last thirty minutes could save him. He knows the forest has some-thing to offer—other than devastation and the end of his life.

He reaches up and dislodges another piece of wood. It falls from the center of the trunk. Chunks of decayed wood tumble down after it. The surface of the trunk is still strong. Because of its angle, water seeped into the trunk and apparently rotted its inside. Absently he pulls another chunk out of the trunk.

And then it occurs to him.

Suddenly he starts digging in the middle of the tree. At first, he's careful, too uncertain to believe he might have found something, some kind of shelter. But in seconds his care dissipates under the real possibility of shelter. His hands are flying. Suddenly he feels energized. The feel of swamp water on his legs evaporates. His hands move with frenetic energy.

It is cartoonish, as though he is a dog burrowing into a hillside at breakneck speed. Hope and energy flood his veins. Lethargy is replaced with a hard rush of adrenaline. In five minutes he has dug out a cave large enough to hold his entire upper body.

He keeps digging. Hands flail, arms pull and throw. As the daylight continues seeping out of the western sky he fashions a deeper hole. There is at least two inches of firm wood surrounding the rotted center. Within fifteen minutes he has used his knife and hands to dig a hole out of the wood wide and long enough to hold almost his entire body. He keeps working, keeps digging.

Just before dark he turns into the woods and forages pine boughs, slashing them off with his blade. He is working quickly now. He has purpose. He has a plan and he is certain it's going to save his life. He gathers three loads of boughs and carries them to the trunk.

He can now wiggle down into the trunk with his head well concealed inside, his legs bent but not folded. He lines the nest with spruce boughs.

It is almost dark, just barely light enough to make his final preparations. He finishes lining the trunk with boughs. There is just enough room to squeeze into his makeshift house. He brings the last bunch in behind him, closing the overhead gap.

It is cold in the tree, dark and enclosed, but he can feel his body heat starting to warm the inside. He has laid enough boughs across the entrance to make a thick mat. He cannot see anything in front of him. There is no light, just the sound of a spare, cold wind. The inside of the tree smells like rich, moldy pine.

He is starting to feel tired now. For another day he has hiked through difficult woods much longer than expected and with entirely different results than those he anticipated—at least when he started. Now he doesn't want to think about it. Now the half-hour adrenaline rush is dissipating as quickly as it rose. A dull ebb of tiredness washes over him. He is well beyond panic, unable to think of much but closing his eyes. And after a few more minutes, totally exhausted, Jason falls asleep.

■ ■ ■

In the middle of the night Jason awakens to howling wind and fierce pain. His calf feels as though it is being lanced. He has little room to move and can only sit and come awake to the pain. He shifts his leg, hoping to assuage the pain.

An enormous windstorm has come out of the sky. He hears a tree topple and fall. It sounds far away, but it must be a large tree. The wind howls and the tops of the trees knock and snap. He has never heard this kind of wind. Even through his pine-bough covering he can hear the blow whipping the tops of the trees.

The pain is back, and when he moves again, slightly, the pain moves, too. There must be a small hole in the side of his shelter with an icy blast spearing through it and cutting into his calf. He shifts again and tries to maneuver a section of tree bough between his leg and the hole. He is only partially successful, but it's enough to give him some respite.

The wind picks up. Jason wonders if the notorious Fourth of July storm from the previous year, the one that blew down a million trees, was kin to this one. Another tree falls, this one closer than the last. More wind, and he hears another tree fall, like a tottering giant in the woods. He cannot believe it, but this one shakes the ground. He can actually feel the ground shudder when it falls. Then another, and another. Giants are falling in the woods. It must be some kind of centennial storm, and he is smack in the middle of it. He is too incredulous to wonder. He realizes that if one of those huge trees topples over on him he'll be crushed. His tree trunk will crumble like an egg.

He closes his eyes and prays, but all he can hear is howling. He asks for deliverance. He doesn't want to be crushed by the forest, though he feels that the woods are doing their best to finish him. But he's a scientist. He is a med student, and he doesn't give much credence to the idea of forest malevolence. He knows there is nothing to be done but lie quietly and try to recover his strength—and hope like hell the storm passes without crushing his narrow home.

Somewhere from inside him a question cannot help but rise unbidden to his lips. *What next*, he wonders. *What in God's name is it going to be next?*

THE DANDY PAT
HUGH FOSBURGH

Until James Dickey published his classic canoe-trip novel, Deliverance, in 1970, I always considered The Sound of White Water *by Hugh Fosburgh to be the best novel on the challenges of heading downriver in a canoe in wild, remote country. First published in 1955,* White Water *earned great critical acclaim. Fosburgh's novel captures all the simple pleasures of canoe-tripping—paddling an interesting river, the camping, the fishing—as experienced by two buddies, Pete and Ben, and their friend Tony, whom they have not seen for fifteen years. They wonder: Can Tony still cut it out here? Their adventure on a fictional river called Big River, which resembles the upper Hudson in New York State (where Fosburgh lived), is spiced up considerably by the challenge of running a rapids. Lives have been lost in these waters, and the three men, each paddling his own canoe, are well aware of the dangers. Most canoe trips are fun, leisurely affairs, with portages around dangerous whitewater stretches. But when you decide to take on the rapids with your canoe, paddle, and skill, your survival is far from assured.*

■ ■ ■

They were breaking their overnight camp on the Stillwater. The three canoes floated broadside to the bank, and each man, sloshing about in the shallow water, was loading his own.

Tony, close to Ben, stopped his work every now and then to see how Ben stowed the watertight bags and roped them down. Up the beach by himself, Pete, stripped to the waist and glistening with sweat, moved about in a deliberate preoccupied way.

Ben and Pete were whistling. Each whistled a different tune, over and over, not hearing it, not thinking about it, just whistling.

Tony was serious, waiting for Ben to look at his loading job and to tell him whether it was all right or not.

Nobody spoke.

They were leaving this lovely peaceful place which had been home for a night, and where they had been companionable and secure. They were going to paddle down to the end of the Stillwater and, way down there around the bend, start into the rapids.

All the night long, awake and sleeping, there had been the dull uneasy groan of the fast water.

■ ■ ■

As they paddled abreast down the last half mile of Stillwater, Ben couldn't help eying Tony. Looking at that thin scrawny body, watching the fierce energy that went into Tony's paddling, Ben was uneasy.

Maybe Tony shouldn't be on this trip. Maybe they were going to be sorry he had come along. Maybe all those jokes about a drowning party were going to be bad jokes. Maybe....

There wasn't a thing to be done about it now, they couldn't turn back. Besides, there wasn't anything to worry about right away. Not for several days at least. Today, they'd go through Cobb's Rifts to the junction with Spruce River, then down the Dandy Pat to the Hell Hole. The Rifts are tricky but there wouldn't be enough water to be dangerous, and the Dandy Pat looked a lot worse than it really was—it was a straightaway run clear to the Hell Hole—so Tony would be all right, he'd get through fine, if he didn't lose his nerve.

Ben doubted that Tony would lose his nerve.

They'd spend a few days fishing at the Hell Hole, and after that there would be plenty of time to start worrying about Tony. So forget it.

Ben didn't forget it. In his mind was the memory of another trip and another man—Sooner Hoffman.

Sooner Hoffman had been a public relations expert, and it had turned out very early in the trip that he was also a blowhard. Somewhat later, he became afraid of the river, going slowly to pieces until he had hysterics there in the rapids above Frenchman's Grief. Ben and Pete had had to take him out of the woods, cross-country, and the whole trip had been a fiasco until they got back on the river by themselves. In retrospect, talking about it with Pete, the whole Sooner Hoffman incident could be made into a hilarious thing, but there hadn't been anything funny about it when it was happening. Nothing at all.

Tony wasn't like Sooner Hoffman, but . . .

They rounded a bend and, of a sudden, the low throbbing moan came pounding upriver to them, and there ahead, where the spruce hills came almost together, was the end of the Stillwater—the zigzag line from shore to shore where the quiet water plunged abruptly from sight, as if pouring over an unseen dam. And beyond was a narrow gorge, dropping away and curving out of sight.

"Let's slow down," said Ben. "We aren't going anywhere in a rush." He stopped paddling, took out his cigarettes, and offered them to Tony. "You want to die like a man, son?"

Tony laughed. "Maybe you'd better blindfold me." He leaned across to get a light from Ben. "It sounds ominous down there."

"It sounds worse than it is," said Ben. "Listen, let me tell you one thing—when you see rapids ahead of you that you don't like the looks of, get out of your canoe and rope it through them. You've got fifty feet of rope there, and that's what it's for. Isn't that right, Pete?"

"That's right," said Pete.

"There isn't any disgrace to roping, see? Get out and rope any time you feel like it. We've got all day and we're not going any place." He hoped that Tony believed him and doubted that he did.

Then he forgot about Tony because the fast water was coming up, just ahead, and he could feel the current begin to clutch at the canoe. He looked at Pete and gestured towards the rapids. "After you, Alphonse."

"*Non, non.*" Pete gave a courtly sweep of his arm. "*Après vous.*"

"All right, we'll put Tony in the middle. You bring up the rear." Ben paddled hard, feeling the nerves flicking in his belly, feeling the vague urge to urinate.

He stood up, the way he always did just before going into fast water, partly to relieve the tension, partly bravado, partly to get a better idea of the course to follow.

He sat down just as the canoe left the Stillwater and was swept into the torrent.

■ ■ ■

Cobb's Rifts are a winding ten-mile staircase—a series of fast rapids stepping down into shallow pools.

Sometimes, when the water is low, getting a canoe through the rapids is a tough frustrating business because then the twisting devious channels are trapped with a myriad boulders that block a clear passage. You can learn to hate those rocks in a very short time.

Today, though, the water was high enough to cover most of the rocks, so Cobb's Rifts was merely a great plaything—a giant liquid roller-coasting toy—put there for the especial benefit and pleasure of Ben and Pete. And they made the most of it. They fancied themselves as expert canoemen, and to manipulate the tricky passage—without hanging up or scraping bottom or shipping water—was proof of it, and they exulted in the proof. They negotiated each rift with breathless abandon, then, in the pool below, drifted carelessly, savoring the thrill of it, while they fished the pockets for bass and waited for Tony to catch up.

Tony got off to a bad start. In the first rift below the Stillwater, he grounded on a rock and nearly turned over. In the confusion of getting off, he shipped a foot of water, then unexpectedly the canoe slipped free of the rock and went wallowing down the rift, out of control. It was luck, and nothing else, that brought it into the pool below without foundering.

Under way again, in the succeeding rifts, Tony had a demoralizing time—there was the feeling that this was all new to him and he couldn't cope with it, he was making a fool of himself, and Ben and Pete were waiting for him down below, they were worried about him, he was spoiling the trip.

He floundered along as best he could.

Then a ridiculous thing happened.

Pete hooked a bass in one of the pools. It was a big vicious-fighting bass so Pete, in a hurry to get it before his canoe was swept into the next rift, called for help from Ben. Ben came close to net it, and together they drifted broadside to the current, intent on the fish, unaware of the drop-off just below. Too late, they saw it, then they were going over it, then their canoes swamped, and they were sputtering and cursing in the water.

Tony, just emerged from the rift above, saw this fiasco, saw the great unconcern with which Pete and Ben took it, so he was grinning when he paddled up, and called out to Ben, "That isn't the way to make your Y in life."

"Don't look so damn smug," said Ben.

On an impulse, Tony turned his canoe and shot into the next rift.

When Ben and Pete finally got under way again, Tony was waiting, sunning himself on a rock, four pools below.

■ ■ ■

They had beached their canoes among the rocks at the bend just below Cobb's Bathtub, and had climbed the rise that gave them a clear view below, and now, with the drowning roar of water in their ears, they were looking at the Dandy Pat. Directly in front, the Spruce came rampaging in from the west to merge with Big River into a brutal wall of water that went surging down through the narrow straightaway gorge.

Nobody spoke for a minute, then Ben was putting a hand on Tony's back and leaning close to shout in his ear, "Right here's where Mister McKeever got cold feet."

Tony laughed abruptly, then he was searching his pockets for a cigarette, and lighting it, and taking deep drags. Then Ben was leaning close again, with one hand on Tony's back for emphasis, while he pointed with the other, and shouted in short disconnected phrases. Tony stood there nodding his head as if he were paying attention and understood everything that Ben was telling him—and looked at the awful flood of water. Ben was pointing to that high spraying crest of water, like a tide rip, that went down the center of the torrent, and telling him that he should get his canoe on the rip and keep it there—the rip looked ugly but it was safe because the water was deepest there, with no rocks. Ben was telling him that all he had to do was stay in the rip and keep his canoe pointed straight downstream—for God's sake don't get crosswise to the current—and there wouldn't be anything to worry about. All Tony had to do was watch where Ben went, and follow exactly, and there wouldn't be anything to it, it would be a snap. Wasn't that right, Pete?

Pete nodded his head.

Ben was finished talking, and was looking very seriously at Tony, then suddenly he was laughing. "Are you ready to give it a whirl?"

Tony heard himself answer, "Let's go," then he was following Ben back to the canoes, and it was like sleepwalking—some external force was making him lift the canoe off the rocks and push it ahead of him into deep water, was making him clamber aboard, snatch up his paddle, and start after Ben. What he was doing wasn't real—the only reality was the shivers in his belly and the clammy coldness and the roar of water, like drowning, and just ahead, coming up fast, the white torrent.

Ben was standing up now, leaning over to paddle, then coming erect, easy and sure, to study the current, then, just at the last, sitting down and giving a dig with his paddle that shot the canoe into the rip.

It's going to be bad, thought Tony, it's going to be awful, something awful is going to happen. What insanity had ever led him to this desperate folly?—then his canoe sliced broadside into the rip and a sheet of water came slapping over the side to lash him in the face. He cursed the water, then he was back-paddling savagely, trying to bring the bow downstream, knowing it wasn't going to work, knowing the torrent was too much for him, but doing it anyway because he couldn't just sit and do nothing, and suddenly, not knowing how he got there, his canoe was on the other side of the rip, pointed upstream. He cursed again, he cursed the satanic water and the canoe that wouldn't do what he wanted, and he cursed himself for his helplessness, then Pete Gay, with that good-time hat cocked on his head, flashed by him in the rip.

The bow of Tony's canoe was being drawn towards the rip again, and Tony watched, fascinated, as it crept into it, then the current grabbed hold and flung it downstream. He made an agonized move to counteract it, and by a miracle the canoe came straight, riding the rip. He sat there rigid, waiting dumbly for the worst to happen, expecting it momentarily, fighting each shift and lurch of the canoe as it dipped and slapped and capered and danced in the mad tumult.

Ahead, as far as he could see, was a plunging rumbling gauntlet, and the shore that was hurtling by was a never-never land. He rode the rip like a nightmare, careening from one horror to the next, and Pete and Ben had deserted him—they were way, way ahead, remote and oblivious.

He was out of the rip again, and ahead, lurking beneath the water, a brown shadowy rock was lying in wait for him. His canoe was knifing straight for it, flying at it. He stabbed at the water with his paddle, and the fickle canoe spun, going sideways again, and then the rock was right there, he was sweeping over it. He flinched, tensing for the crash. There was no crash, and when he dared look, the rock was disappearing upstream. He cursed again, for being such a fool, wrenched the canoe around, and was back in the rip.

It was desperate, and he was alone, and there was no end. He was trapped in this cataract, and every foot was an ambush for his flimsy ridiculous craft. If he escaped one disaster it didn't matter, another was waiting for him, and another. Hundreds. Miles of them. Sooner or later. . . .

He crouched there, exhausted, cold-sweating, working with desperate frenzy to hold the canoe in the rip, and then, suddenly, there ahead, waiting in a little side eddy, waving and shouting encouragement, was Pete.

Tony smiled tightly as he swept by.

He wasn't alone any more. Ben was there, going down just ahead (he must have waited too), and Pete was behind. Maybe the worst was behind. He'd been lucky and maybe his luck would hold. Ben had said the rapids looked worse than they were, and maybe Ben was right. Ben had said to follow where he went, and it would be a snap.

Tony watched Ben head into a vicious fall of water, then Ben was in it and lost from sight in the spray, then he reappeared below, riding easily, as if nothing had happened. Tony followed exactly as Ben had gone, then he was in the fall and out again, safe, and by God it wasn't luck that had got him through, he had done it himself.

He took a huge breath—the first good breath he had taken in an eternity—and eased the cramps from his legs, then he was digging in with the paddle to exert his new-found control over the canoe, making it swing just the way he wanted.

Behind, so close Tony could hear it above the rush of water, Pete was roaring out some wild ecstatic song.

■ ■ ■

You know what real fear is—it's like a cold serum that seeps through, numbing your body, petrifying your senses, making you almost sick with helpless petulant rage.

And then suddenly it's gone—something happens and the fear evaporates like a fog, it just isn't there any more, you're free of it—and then you feel better than you ever felt in your life, lightheaded, drunk with confidence. You could whip the world.

And you know what speed—real dangerous speed—can do to you. It's the same whether you're hedge-hopping a fighter, or racing a car on a winding road, or galloping a team of horses down a skidway, or taking a canoe through a flood of water—you live in the immediate tumultuous instant; there is no past, and the future is there before you can see it or reckon with it. There is just the heart-stopping thought-less whirling cataract of speed.

That's the way Tony Farr came down the Dandy Pat—drunk with the simple tumultuous excitement of speed. Ben was there ahead and Tony must follow Ben exactly. There was the rip and he must stay in the rip. There was the roar of water, and above the roar was Pete's crazy song.

You do it your way and I'll do it a-new,
The bugger who did it last time will ne'er
do it noo.

Then the river angled around a high bluff, and ahead, plunging steeply, was a narrow white-spraying chute. Ben was swallowed up in it, then Tony was engulfed, and unex-pectedly, Pete was right beside him, not three feet away, pad-dling like mad and roaring his song. Side by side, they made the careening ride, then the canoes erupted from the chute into a deep black smooth-flowing pool, and the crashing roar of water melted away behind.

Ben was there, drifting in the slack. "Welcome to the Hell Hole," he said.

A WALK IN THE PARK

JILL FREDSTON

*Avalanches are something most skiers and snow-country hikers and climbers
don't need to worry about. They only exist in news headlines proclaiming
tragic loss of life in remote backcountry regions. Nevertheless, they are
out there, and they kill without warning. What's it like to be swept off a
mountainside by a wall of snow, buried under the sliding wave of white? Can
you breathe? Can you survive until the rescuers find you? How long can you
last? Does it hurt?* With Snowstruck: In the Grip of Avalanches, *author Jill
Fredston recounts some of the rescue operations she has undertaken while
living in the active avalanche zones of Alaska, both those ending in joy and
those ending in tragedy. Here she takes us right to* Ground Zero, *where
deadly avalanches buried the unsuspecting.*

. . .

I noticed him in the crowded theater right away. He was trim
and handsome, with an athlete's energy and a flashbulb smile
that made him seem more a boy than a man nearing forty.
As he sat laughing with his friends, waiting for the performance to begin, he kept tipping his wheelchair into grace-
ful wheelies. "Look," I said, nudging Doug. "Isn't that Nick
Coltman?" When we had last seen him, he lay broken and
freezing, straddling the wafer-thin line between now and
before, before and after, here and gone.

Born in England and raised in Australia and New
Hampshire, Coltman was a skilled outdoorsman who had

traveled the world for adventure and was accustomed to spending fifty days a winter on skis. But on the day he triggered a tiny avalanche with disproportionate consequences, he wasn't exploring the high mountains of Nepal or etching ski turns across the face of a remote Alaskan glacier. He had only gone for a short walk in what was essentially his backyard.

If the day had played out as so many had before, Coltman would have put his dog back into the car after a two-hour jaunt and driven into town to spend the rest of the afternoon with his wife, Maggie. If he could rewrite the day, he might elect not to go hiking, or choose a different route, or succeed in having his ice axe find purchase on the icy slope. If he could rewrite the day, his life would be the way it always had been, and his future would be as he had planned. But though we must pretend otherwise in order to function, none of us can know the script for any day.

I also spied John Stroud in the theater that night. Although they didn't know each other, Nick Coltman and John Stroud could easily have been friends. Both were tempted north to Alaska in the early 1990s. They lived within a few miles of each other. Both were in their mid-thirties when avalanches interrupted their lives. Both loved to hike, climb, and ski the same mountains. Both loved to come home with stories, which Coltman would tell in the quick, ready style of his trade—he is a newspaper publisher—while Stroud, a computer wizard, might need more coaxing. In describing the avalanches that snared each of them, Coltman might flash his easy grin, while Stroud's more cautious smile would likely be lost in his beard. Both, however, would say they were lucky.

■　■　■

Seven miles east of downtown Anchorage is the trailhead for Flattop, the most popular mountain in Alaska. If someone scrambles up only one mountain in the state, it is likely to be the 3,510-foot peak, which lies at the accessible edge of Chugach State Park. If you look north from the summit on a clear day, you can see Alaska's highest mountain, 20,320-foot Mount McKinley (also known as Denali), crowding the sky 150 miles away. A procession of increasingly tall peaks and expansive glaciers beckon from the west. Moments from the parking lot, you leave the last "bonsai" forests of wind-wizened hemlock trees and emerge onto open tundra. Runners flog themselves into shape by using Flattop as a StairMaster, and families picnic on its flanks. Hikers congregate on Flattop's summit to shiver through the longest night of the year in December and to cheer the midnight sun in June. People get married on Flattop, and they die there.

More mountain rescue missions are launched to Flattop and the surrounding "front range" areas of Chugach State Park than to anywhere else in the vastness of Alaska. The frequency of accidents in the front range is often attributed to the density of the surrounding population, and certainly, without people or our trappings, there is no exposure to danger and, therefore, no hazard. Familiarity and accessibility, however, inflate the problem by making us complacent. The mountains don't behave any differently just because they are close to town. "The most dangerous thing," says Jerry Lewanski, superintendent of Chugach State Park, "is that the area is so close to civilization. There's no transition zone. You don't spend hours in your car driving to get there. There's no time to psychologically prepare."

■   ■   ■

Nick Coltman woke on Saturday, November 11, 2000, with no intention of becoming the front-page story in the *Anchorage Daily News* or the alternative weekly newspaper he cofounded, the *Anchorage Press*. He hadn't even planned to take his ritual dash up Flattop with his chocolate Lab, Boozer, until he saw the sun—a precious commodity in Alaska. A run of dreary days had given way to a serenely beautiful late fall morning, with no wind and temperatures a notch above freezing. Two days home from Hawaii, Coltman yearned for the snow he might find at the top of the mountain.

Dressed lightly enough to move quickly, Coltman veered off the trail about a thousand feet below the summit and traversed into a network of long, rocky, fingerlike gullies. Asked later why he had chosen the cold, shadowed route over direct sun, he replied with trademark jauntiness, "There are always fewer people on the dark side." To avoid a hiker descending with two dogs, Coltman swung even farther left than usual, though still on turf he and Boozer knew well.

It had done nothing but pour in Anchorage the previous three days. But toward the end of the storm, the temperature near Flattop's summit had cooled enough to chill the precipitation into freezing rain that greased the rocks with ice before changing to dry snow. Strong winds had stripped exposed ridges bare and blown the snow into shallow drifts not much deeper than six inches. In most places the snow was either nonexistent or so thin that, with every kicked step, Coltman's hiking boots stubbed icy ground.

The crux of Coltman's route was the last several hundred feet below the summit where the gully narrows, steepens, and snakes into a bend. He took a few strides into a slightly deeper snow patch to which he took an instant dislike. "I'd seen similar conditions in this spot before," he says, "and always been able to traverse onto a rock ramp and avoid the danger zone. This time I did something I'd never done before. I looked below me and thought, *Ooh, I wouldn't want to fall down that*. I turned toward the safety of the rock, put my ice axe in, and that's when I saw the crack go."

The slab that dish-plated out from under Coltman was no larger than a Ping-Pong table and barely three inches deep. "There was no sound that I remember. At first it was like riding a pillow. Then I started tumbling, ass over teacup, and I knew I was in for it," Coltman later told one of his own reporters.

▪ ▪ ▪

Yielding to the temptation of new snow and sunshine, John Stroud skipped work the afternoon of March 28, 2002, to ski in Chugach State Park. With his two dogs and a friend, Skip Repetto, he drove a half hour from Anchorage into the south fork of Eagle River, a majestic valley where houses grip the lower skirts of Alplike peaks. Parking near the end of the road, Stroud and Repetto fastened mohair skins onto their telemark skis for traction and began climbing toward a ridge that cupped three sizable widemouthed snow-filled bowls. Though both men had taken avalanche training before coming to Alaska and recognized that the terrain could produce avalanches under the right conditions, they didn't know that the name of their chosen playground was Three Bowl Path.

Their first downhill run was perfect. For safety's sake, they skied one at a time, each skier disappearing behind a rooster tail of powder. At the bottom, as Stroud and Repetto admired the fluid calligraphy of their tracks, they couldn't help but decide to make another run. This time they chose a different line that led them into the gut of the southernmost bowl.

As with Coltman's accident, there were a lot of ifs to this afternoon. If Stroud and Repetto hadn't tried to squeeze in a few more turns near the bottom of their second run by crossing a V-shaped creek drainage and traversing onto a north-facing slope, they might never have triggered the avalanche. Nor might it have happened if Stroud, maintaining a safe distance behind Repetto, had heeded his friend's warning to stay put because the snow didn't feel right. If Stroud's dogs hadn't dropped into the gully ahead of him, tempting him to follow, there might not have been enough weight in the gully bottom to provide a trigger—or, alternatively, only Repetto might have been caught.

People can grow pretty unstable if kept in dark, cold places all their lives (which is why so many Alaskans take winter breaks in Hawaii). The same goes for layers of snow that lurk in shadowed areas like north-facing slopes. The instant Repetto crossed to a different slope aspect, his ski poles began sinking into a seemingly bottomless layer beneath the new powder. Repetto was perched atop a house of cards. He shouted a quick warning to Stroud and started looking for the fastest way out.

To appreciate the precariousness of Repetto's perch, you must put your head inside the snowpack. Snow appears to be a solid substance, but it is more like lace, a delicate lattice of frozen water and airspaces filled with water vapor molecules. Newly fallen powder is made up of only 5 to 15 percent water, while the rest is air. Even old settled snow packed to the density of a sidewalk is more than one-half air. The undercover agents of change are water vapor molecules and temperature. If a strong temperature difference exists within or between layers, as is often true on shaded slopes early in the winter when the snow cover is thin or during very cold periods, the molecules migrate from the relatively warm top of one snow grain to the colder underside of the grain above. Rather than creating bonds between the grains, the water vapor accretes to make each grain bigger. The trend is to build increasingly large, blocky, poorly connected grains known as facets or, because of the similarity in texture, sugar snow. The longer the temperature gradient exists and the process is allowed to continue, the larger, more sugary, and more persistent the grains.

Faceted snow, in any stage of development, can be a deadly weak layer. In the grains' most advanced form, when they have progressed beyond angled corners and simple striations to form very large hollow cups about half the size of a pea with glittery jewel-like facets visible to the naked eye, they are called depth hoar. As director of the Canadian Avalanche Association Clair Israelson observes, "Depth hoar is like having your crazy aunt come for a visit. You never know when she is going to snap."

Stroud's dogs, malamute-huskies, were no feather dusters—each of them tipped the scales at more than a hundred pounds. The stress of the two wallowing dogs, combined with that of the two men, was too much for the weak depth hoar in the bottom of the gully. It collapsed with a declarative *whumph*. The collapse began around the men's skis and radiated in all directions. If they'd had the luxury to stand their ground and watch, Stroud and Repetto would have seen the snow surface physically drop an inch as one collapse caused another, then another. As the failure of the weak layer under the slab dominoed uphill, it would have looked as though waves were surfing up the slope with the slow, ominous roll of an ocean swell ahead of a storm. The collapses propagated a full five hundred vertical feet before a slab more than two feet deep and a quarter of a mile wide peeled free. Stroud and Repetto might as well have pulled bricks from the ground floor of a fifty-story skyscraper, only to see the building disintegrate.

Repetto had celebrated his thirty-eighth birthday the night before, but now it seemed he was going to die. Clipped at the heels by the onrushing avalanche, he urged speed from his skis, trying to traverse the eddy line that divided sliding snow from stationary snow. He's almost made it when he was flipped backward into the froth. Twice he tried to pick himself up, and on the second attempt, he stayed upright long enough to cross the eddy line to safety. He looked down toward the creek bottom where snow from the three sides of the bowl was converging and was sure that he had just killed his ski partner. The channel was churning with huge waves of snow that looked like the wildest of whitewater on an unnavigable river. Somewhere in this turbulence, Stroud and his dogs were drowning.

On the opposite edge of the gully, Stroud thought he was far enough to the side to escape the avalanche when a second wave of snow coming from a different direction caught him around the knees. Blocked from safety by the low but smooth and sloping gully wall and caged by ski bindings that did not release, Stroud felt as if he were wearing concrete shoes. As he clawed at the gully's purchaseless walls, the laminar flow of snow debris rose to his wait, his chest, and then his shoulders, drawing him inexorably under, until snow topped his head and locked him into darkness.

Nick Coltman hurtled a punishing six hundred feet down a rocky slope that was only marginally dusted with snow and steep enough to be rated expert terrain at a ski area. When he came to a precarious rest, his head was downhill and bleeding profusely. He couldn't take a breath without feeling searing pain. Nor could he move his legs. His dog, Boozer, was nowhere to be seen. At first Coltman thought he was buried to his waist, but when he saw his legs twisted like pipe cleaners on the snow surface, he thought, *No, I'm paralyzed. That complicates things.*

Coltman knew that death was certain if he couldn't reach the cell phone in the small pack still strapped to his broken back. His hat and gloves had been knocked off in the fall, and most of his backpack's contents—a few extra warm clothes, water, and snack food—had also free-fallen when the torn bottom, patched and stitched together with dental floss years before, succumbed to the rocks. But the cell phone was zippered into a separate top pouch.

Backcountry travelers have increasingly relied upon cell phones to extricate them from emergency situations that could have been prevented by packing good judgment. I recently returned from the nighttime rescue of two skiers carried onto a steep brushy mountainside by an avalanche. They used a cell phone to call for rescue, but when I spotted them from a helicopter with the aid of a searchlight, they were standing and waving energetically. I could see no sign of debilitating injuries and, with no landing zones anywhere nearby, I knew the process of extrication would be hard, slow, and cold. The easiest, fastest solution, I told them by cell phone, was for them to walk downhill. Once they started moving, they reached the road in twenty minutes.

Accustomed to being self-reliant, Coltman hadn't brought his cell phone for safety. Like Boozer, the phone was simply always with him. Usually, he'd call his wife from Flattop's summit, and they would spin their plans for the day.

"I remember only bits and pieces of the accident," says Coltman. "I remember just the first second or two of the fall. I remember going fast. I remember thinking I had to get to the cell phone. I knew that I wasn't going to stay conscious long. I have no idea how I got the pack off my back."

Coltman's 911 emergency call was recorded right before noon, probably less than three minutes after his fall. It is remarkable for its coherence. He told the dispatcher his name, that he'd been caught in an avalanche on the north side of Flattop, and that he couldn't feel his legs. After giving his cell phone number and precise information about his location, Coltman had no choice but to sever the connection to save battery power.

In *Deep Survival*, a book that explores why some people live through ordeals that kill others, Laurence Gonzales writes: "The maddening thing for someone with a Western scientific turn of mind is that it's not what's in your pack that separates the quick from the dead. It's not even what's in your mind. Corny as it sounds, it's what's in your heart." Coltman could not have survived without the cell phone, but for most people it would have made little difference. They simply would not have had the heart to endure being so broken and so cold for so long.

Willing a helicopter into the air, Coltman lay on the slope, growing ominously colder and murmuring, "Oh, help me, help me, help me," to no one in particular. From his upside-down position, he spotted Boozer several hundred feet downhill and called to him. Boozer, his right rear leg cut to the bone, left his own trail of blood as he limped to Coltman's side.

Maggie Balean worried when she didn't receive her husband's usual call from the top of the mountain. Twenty minutes after his 911 call, she dialed his cell. "I can still hear our conversation distinctly," says Balean. "I said, 'Where are you?' and Nick said, 'I've had an accident and I'm paralyzed.'" He explained that he'd called 911 and couldn't talk long because he needed to save the phone's batteries. "He told me that he loved me and then he hung up, and I started going crazy."

The response to 911 calls for accidents in Chugach State Park is sometimes bungled because while there are almost too many agencies close at hand, few are capable of mounting an effective rescue in rough terrain even a short distance beyond the end of the road. Coltman's call, though, was like the single match that sparks a wildfire. By 12:10 Alaska State Parks, the Anchorage Police Department, and the Anchorage Fire Department all had crews in the parking lot at the trailhead, and a request for assistance had been made to the Alaska Mountain Rescue Group, which initiated a phone and pager callout to gather a volunteer response team. Helicopters were being summoned from more than one direction.

■ ∶ ■

John Stroud was entombed so completely that the only part of his body he could move, albeit almost imperceptibly, was the index finger of his left hand. He couldn't even open his eyes. His first reaction was to yell. He yelled for his dogs, whom he knew would find him if they weren't buried. He yelled for Repetto, whom he had seen get caught but prayed had reached the edge of the avalanche. He yelled until he realized that he'd better save his energy and his breath. With little emotion, he said his good-byes and faded into sleep induced by too little oxygen and a glut of carbon dioxide. He didn't even have time for the full weight of sadness for what he was leaving behind to settle upon him.

An avalanche victim stands a much greater chance of survival if some part of his body or a piece of gear that is still attached to him is protruding from the snow. Playing dead may work for brown bear attacks, but it is the wrong strategy when caught in an avalanche. Victims need to put up a fierce fight as they are carried downslope and use swimming motions to stay near the surface—any stroke is worth trying, even the dog paddle. Avalanches most often kill by suffocation, though broken necks and other forms of fatal trauma have become increasingly common as people jump into every more ruthless terrain. There is air even in dense avalanche debris, but it is unattainable if the victim's mouth and nose are plugged with snow. Even if the victim can draw a breath, his exhalations will begin to make any available air less accessible by coating the snow surface around his mouth with ice. We always excavate carefully around a victim's face to determine whether there is an ice mask, for that is an indication of how long he lived under the snow; thick ice masks are hauntingly disturbing to find.

Poisoned by their own carbon dioxide emissions, most victims begin to lose consciousness within four minutes, which is a good thing, as they will use air at a slower rate. Brain damage may set in after eight minutes. Within twenty-five minutes, half of all completely buried victims die; within thirty-five minutes, almost three-quarters are dead. To have any chance of living longer, victims must have some sort of air pocket, perhaps one created by throwing an arm in front of their face as they were buried. A victim buried faceup rather than facedown is twice as likely to survive because a larger airspace is created in front of his mouth as his head melts the snow. People rarely survive burials deeper than six feet, not only because they take longer to find and dig out (and are thus more vulnerable to both asphyxiation and hypothermia), but also because they have greater compressive weight upon them.

No helicopters were on the way to help Stroud, and no rescuers had been summoned. Stroud's dogs were dead and would not be found for months. His only chance of survival lay on the slender shoulders of Skip Repetto, who at that moment was preparing to flee.

Repetto was worried that the two other bowls could release and sluice into the same gully bottom, burying him before he had the chance to find Stroud. He could see houses below him. They were tantalizingly close, and Repetto calculated that it would take less than five minutes to ski to them and seek help. Even a few people could speed up the search considerably, and he was urgently aware that time was the enemy. Repetto, though, didn't want to "ski off the mountain alone." In the darkest corners of his mind, he knew that if he chased the mirage of help, his friend would die. He turned his back to the houses.

Stroud's only lifeline to the surface was the invisible electromagnetic signal being transmitted by three tiny triple-A batteries inside the avalanche beacon strapped to his chest. The use of avalanche beacons, which were invented in 1968, has burgeoned since the 1980s, paralleling the boom in backcountry winter recreation and a concomitant surge in accidents. About the size of a television remote control, a beacon—or avalanche rescue transceiver, as it is also known—offers the best chance of finding a buried person alive. Even so, the official statistics are discouraging: two out of three people wearing beacons are dug out dead. This ratio is misleading, as we are more likely to hear about the fatal accidents than the close calls in which one friend locates another with a beacon, digs him out, and they go home with little fanfare. But the reality is that even those wearing beacons can break their necks, be unable to expand their chests enough to breathe, or run out of air long before they are shoveled free. Beacons, like cell phones, can even contribute to accidents by making us feel safer. If we have the attitude that we'll be okay if something goes wrong, then we are more likely to act in ways that increase the likelihood of something going wrong.

A transmitting beacon emits its signal in flux lines shaped like the wings of a butterfly. The distance at which this signal can be detected by another beacon switched to receive generally varies between fifty and a hundred feet, though beacon manufacturers offer more optimistic numbers. Repetto thought that Stroud hadn't been carried very far, and he expected to have a slow, tough climb back up the debris-choked gully. He surged with hope when he hustled within range of Stroud's signal in ninety seconds. Flashing red lights on the digital display of his beacon directed him in a gentle arc along one of the flux lines, closing the distance. Within three minutes Repetto was standing almost on top of Stroud's grave.

Sweating and panting, Repetto heaved off his pack and screwed together his ski poles, which were designed to double as an avalanche probe. It can be tough to know what you are probing. Springy bushes, a layer of slush, or muddy ground can have the same spongy feel as a body. This time, though, Repetto only had to probe a few times before he was sure that he was striking Stroud's body three or four feet below him.

Repetto grabbed the small aluminum shovel off his pack and began hurling snow. With a shovel, moving a cubic meter of snow—roughly the equivalent volume of a household refrigerator—takes at least ten minutes. Without a shovel, it takes five times as long. Repetto dug for ten minutes, and when he leaned into the bottom of the cone-shaped hole, worried because he couldn't see any sign of Stroud, he heard his friend grunting. It was an *ugghhh-ugghhh-ugghhh* cavemanlike sound that suggested stress, if not pain—but Stroud was alive! Fueled by emotion, Repetto shoveled well beyond the point of fatigue. Pouring sweat, he dug and dug and dug through soft debris that kept sliding back into the hole. He dug even as Stroud ceased grunting and he couldn't hear any breathing noises at all. He dug until he was standing in a long, almost chest-high trench. The digging was taking too long—fifteen, twenty, twenty-five minutes. Repetto was working too hard to have an exact sense of time, but he knew that with every extra minute of burial, Stroud's chances of survival were plummeting exponentially. Repetto's arms and back burned, and his hope was ebbing.

Stroud's head came into view first, like a dark atoll in a frozen sea. Stroud was unconscious, and he didn't appear to be breathing. From his knees, Repetto reached down, pulled Stroud's bluish face up, and scooped his fingers into his friend's mouth to clear it of snow. Like a balky engine, Stroud sputtered back to life with a rough cough. It would take another ten minutes for him to regain consciousness, and twenty more minutes of deliberate digging to free the rest of his body. If Stroud had been buried even a minute or two longer, he likely would have died.

. . .

Doug and I live one ridge over from Flattop, less than fifteen minutes of fast driving away from the trailhead parking lot. As is not unusual on a beautiful Saturday, both phone lines at home had rung simultaneously—one call from Alaska State Parks, who contact us as soon as they hear the word *avalanche*, and the other from the Alaska Mountain Rescue Group, with whom we have worked for decades. Both conveyed the same message: *MOVE!* We were told that a fast response was especially imperative because the avalanche victim who had summoned help was buried headfirst to his waist. Grabbing our rescue packs, we stampeded out the door in whatever we were wearing, which in Doug's case was dubiously adequate canvas carpenter pants and rubber boating boots. I was better prepared as I'd just returned from climbing the ridge behind our house. Only when we were in the car did we have time to wonder how the victim could have made a cell phone call if his head was buried.

As a kid, I loved playing the game of telephone, where a message was whispered from one person to another. By the time it came full circle, it rarely bore more than a trace of its original meaning. The initial information about the location and particulars of an accident almost always becomes similarly garbled. You might think you are going to look for a missing hiker at a certain trailhead when, in fact, the mission involves the evacuation of a hunter who has fallen off a cliff in an entirely different drainage. In this case Coltman's message that he couldn't feel his legs had somehow mutated into a headfirst burial. But we didn't know this yet. As we sped out of our valley, we passed two friends who looked miffed when we didn't stop to talk. "Avalanche! Flattop!" I yelled out the window, noting their surprise that there could be an avalanche with snow not even ankle deep on the ground.

A flaming-red Lifeguard helicopter from one of the local hospitals was in the parking lot when we arrived. It had already circled the north side of Flattop and spotted Coltman, but now the pilot was waiting for us to assess the remaining avalanche hazard before ferrying in rescuers. "There's only room for one of you," shouted a paramedic over the clamor of the turning rotors. I nodded a *Go!* to Doug, who knows Flattop's every contour and can run down steep slopes faster than I can. With ducked heads, the two of them bolted toward the open helicopter door. I turned to the rescuer next to me and shouted, "Who?" I didn't know Nick, but his name resonated; it took me until later that evening to register that he called us periodically to get avalanche condition updates for his newspaper's ski column.

The avalanche hazard call was refreshingly simple for Doug to make. All the snow in the gully had slid, stripping the upper slope to a bed of icy rocks. Like Stroud, Coltman had left catlike scrape marks in the ice, an eerie record of his fight to slow his fall with his fingertips after his ice axe was wrenched away. From the broad, level landing pad of Flattop's summit, Doug blitzed hundreds of vertical feet down the mountain, still thinking that Coltman might be suffocating.

If Nick Coltman had in fact been buried, he might at least have benefited from snow's insulating qualities. As it was, lying bareheaded and thinly clad on snow in below-freezing temperatures, he was losing heat so quickly that hypothermia might kill him before his other injuries could. He was also in danger of rag-dolling farther down the treacherously slick slope. Coltman's arms were flung Christlike across the slope, and Doug, the first rescuer to reach him, had to pry the cell phone from his white frostbitten fingertips. Doug says, "The only good thing about the horribly uncomfortable position Nick was in, upside down on a 35-degree skating rink, was that the increased flow of blood to his brain probably helped keep him conscious long enough to make the call for help."

Coltman recalls, "I knew Doug by reputation. I relaxed the instant he introduced himself, thinking, *Oh good, I'm going to be okay.*" But until additional help arrived, Doug could only do so much. Keeping up a constant patter, Doug worked to assess Coltman's injuries, slow the rate at which he was cooling with heat packs and extra clothes, and anchor him to the slope. Doug knew that Coltman's rescue would be measured in hours, not minutes. He says, "I told Nick straight out, 'Look, you're going to have to be real tough and fight like hell to stay alive. Otherwise, you're probably not going to make it.' Really, I was preaching to the choir because I don't think I've ever met anyone with more willpower."

The fire department medics wisely descended more slowly than Doug and arrived ten minutes behind him. Once on site, they were responsible for trying to keep Coltman's injuries from killing him. The Lifeguard helicopter was useful for ferrying me and other reinforcements uphill, but without a winch, it couldn't help with the urgent task of evacuating

Coltman—the terrain was far too inhospitable for it to land nearby. Coltman was a long mile from the parking lot and in such a fragile state that he probably would not survive the painful and time-consuming process of being lowered to gentler terrain. Coltman's only chance lay in a helicopter equipped with a sling hoist that could pluck him to safety.

The National Guard's 210th Air Rescue Squadron had been requested shortly after Coltman's plight became known. But as we gently moved Coltman into a rescue litter and onto the more level platform we'd hacked from the frozen slope with ice axes, we heard by radio that the Pave Hawk helicopter was "forty-five minutes out." For Coltman, time compressed into a blur and the details were lost. For those of us watching him grow colder, become less lucid, and struggle harder for breath while Boozer jealously guarded his side, time elongated and began to grate.

The welcome noise of the approaching Pave Hawk rebounded off the valley's walls until it sounded as though an army of helicopters was in the sky. Down below, our team of nearly a dozen rescuers hunkered protectively around Coltman like musk ox. We knew that as the helicopter moved into a hover overhead, the freezing rotor wash would reach a hundred miles per hour and could easily rip us from an icy perch so tenuous that we could barely keep from falling even when standing still. Looking toward the open door of the helicopter from my position by Coltman's head, I saw two pararescue jumpers, more commonly known as PJs, being lowered by winch at the same time. There are fewer than 350 PJs in the United States. PJs can't leap tall buildings in a single bound, but trained to rescue anyone from anywhere, they come closer than just about any other mortals. These are the kind of guys who think nothing of scuba diving and parachuting in the same afternoon, and who wear watches the diameter of Coke bottles on their well-shaped forearms.

The pilot had to hold a high hover to keep the chopper's rotors clear of the slope and to avoid becoming disoriented in the whiteout created by the rotor wash. As the length of cable increased, the two PJs began to spin like figure skaters, with sickeningly fast revolutions. Worse—for us at least— they were going to land right on top of our huddle rather than safely to the side. Most of our team, with heads down, hoods up, and ears deafened by the helicopter's roar, didn't hear Doug's bellowed warning. One rescuer took a glancing blow to his helmeted head from a spinning PJ's outstretched legs, and another was knocked a short distance downhill. It could easily have been catastrophic, with all of us and Coltman cartwheeling down the mountain. "Sorry to drop in on you like this," quipped one of the PJs as he stood woozily to his feet.

The relentless rotor wash transformed the slope around us as though turning the clock back on the seasons, blowing away all the snow except for the denser lobe of avalanche debris. Coltman's litter was clipped to the slender steel cable within moments. Dangling and twisting as it was winched across a cleft of blue sky, the stretcher diminished into a black dot and disappeared into the dark maw of the helicopter. Three hours after taking his last step, Coltman was on his way to the hospital.

By the time Coltman reached the emergency room, he was dangerously hypothermic, with a core temperature of 87 degrees and an irregular heartbeat. If he'd been two degrees colder, he likely would have been in a coma. "I don't remember the emergency room at all," he says. "I'm told that they wrapped me in a warming blanket and that when they began pumping warm fluids through every orifice, I became quite vocal." In fact, Coltman began joking with his army of attendants and speaking in perfectly comprehensible Chinese to Maggie, who hails from Taiwan. (Yes, he was fluent before the accident.) His body, though, was in pieces. He had a host of broken ribs, both of his lungs were collapsed and filled with blood, and his spine was cracked in two places, leaving him without feeling below his waist and rendering him paraplegic.

· · ·

When John Stroud regained consciousness, even as he shivered uncontrollably, he thought obsessively of his dogs. They had always gleefully joined him, eager to do whatever he was doing. They were family and, since his recent split with his wife, his sole roommates. It tortured Stroud to think that he had brought them into this dangerous place and killed them. He and Repetto, though, were in no shape to do more than hurl unanswered cries into the darkening sky and limp off the mountain.

That night, a shaky Stroud telephoned friends and family. One of the people he called was Don Zimmerman, the only other Alaska employee of the software company for which Stroud works. Stroud described the avalanche in detail, warning his colleague that similarly treacherous conditions must be lurking nearby. Three days later, on a beautiful Easter Sunday, Zimmerman and his stepfather, along with two more dogs, died in an avalanche in the neighboring valley, near a peak named Mount Magnificent.

Stroud's avalanche was orders of magnitude bigger than Coltman's, and yet he walked away essentially uninjured. If

Coltman had traversed only one or two feet higher on the slope, he never would have triggered the avalanche. The slab that caught him was no thicker than a pizza box.

Just as little slabs on big slopes should command our respect, so must relatively large avalanches on little slopes. In Alaska two soldiers were killed on a creek bank with a vertical relief of only thirty-six feet. Two children near Denali National Park—where visitors from all over the world come to marvel at the immensity of the Alaska Range—were completely buried when playing on a hill no higher than fifteen feet. Similar stories abound from avalanche-prone places around the globe and even from milder, less mountainous climes caught unaware by a rare snowstorm.

Every accident, of any kind, is preceded by a chain of events or errors, but each is set into motion at one irreversible moment. Until that moment the accident might have been prevented. Darkness, an icy road, high speed, an inexperienced driver, and a heavy foot on the brake can conspire to create dangerous circumstances, but a car crash might not be inevitable until the car starts to skid. In Stroud's accident the irreversible moment announced itself with a *whumph* as soon as Stroud joined his dogs and his friend in the gully. For Coltman, the irreversible moment came when he stepped onto the slab. Asked in an interview by his own paper, the *Anchorage Press*, whether he'd made a mistake, Coltman answered, "Not really. If I had thought to myself, *Shit, I really shouldn't be going up this*, and I'd gone ahead anyway, then yes, I would tell you I made a mistake. But that's not what happened. The instant I realized I was in a bad spot, I tried to get out of it. Unfortunately, that was an instant too late."

Avalanches are perceived as the equivalent of a drunk

driver, barreling through an intersection and nailing innocent pedestrians. Whether small like Coltman's or abnor-
mally big, like the billion-pounder in Williwaw Path, they
are frequently met with incredulity and portrayed as freak
events. The harsher truth is that as long as people live, work,
or play in the mountains, avalanche accidents are certain.
Roughly 95 percent of the avalanches that catch those at
play are triggered by the victims. These victims are typically
experienced, as were Coltman and Stroud, rather than rank
beginners. If we can predict that these accidents will happen
every year, can we more specifically predict where, or when,
or to whom?

When the police apprehend a driver suspected to be
drunk, they request that he exit the car and walk a straight
line; if he can't, he is considered inebriated. Of course, the
test is not foolproof, because some drunks can walk straight.
The thin line that tethers us all to life is invisible, far from
straight, and famously fickle. It is a line we are constantly
walking yet are only allowed to stray across once.

At the rehabilitation center where Nick Coltman was sent
to adjust to his new body, he met patients who had become
paralyzed as the result of doing nothing more dramatic than
wrestling with their kids in the front yard or tripping on the
sidewalk. How can we tiptoe through the mountains—or
even through everyday life—and manage to stay on the safe
side of a line we can't see? How can we stay aware of the thin
line without letting fear of it paralyze us?

There is a moment toward the end of some avalanche
searches when I feel as though I am suspended above the thin
line with a clear, unbroken view of both sides. It's almost as if I
can still see the ribbon stretching across the finish line, though

I know a runner has just come crashing through. The result of the race hasn't yet been announced or at least spread very far, so it is a very private moment. I had such a flash on the flanks of Mount Magnificent after we'd dug out Don Zimmerman and his stepfather, along with the stiff bodies of their two dogs.

It was a warm day, with sparkling mountains etched into a sapphire sky. With the search over, all the hustle had drained out of our actions, and we'd gained some mental space by zipping the two men into misleadingly cheerful yellow body bags so that their faces were no longer visible. I sat on my pack amid a cocoon of rescue friends and watched a body bag sway beneath the helicopter that was ferrying the victims to a destination of grief. I still knew little about the dead snowshoers except for their names, and I hadn't yet met their families. For a short soothing interlude, while I waited to be one of the last off the mountain, I was free to soak in the sun and let myself be washed by laughter and conversation that was life affirming rather than irreverent. Soon enough this innocent interval would be replaced by the flashing lights of emergency vehicles in a crowded parking lot, microphones thrust into my face, and the wrenching questions of families who wanted to know how the day had gone so wrong. One of the wives would ask me if her husband's eyes had been open and whether I thought he had lived long enough to know he was going to die. Doug and I would go home and try to pick up our lives wherever we had dropped them; by nighttime, I knew, the faces of the victims would intrude upon our dreams. But for now I was at rare liberty just to be.

.   .   .

Don Zimmerman's memorial service was held the week after Easter, on yet another ruthlessly sunny day. From the church parking lot, Stroud could see both the valley where he had almost died and the mountain where Zimmerman had not been so lucky. "I couldn't help but wonder why I survived and they didn't," he says, in a voice husky with embarrassment. "It was a strange feeling. I didn't feel shame. I didn't feel bad. I wasn't happy. Mostly I was just struck by the oddness of being alive."

A week or two later, at the request of his employer, Stroud went to Zimmerman's house to collect some work-related material. The house was high on the mountainside, commanding the entrance to the valley of Zimmerman's death. "I stood at the picture window with Don's widow's mother," Stroud says, "and she told me over and over again how much she hated snow. And all I could think about was how beautiful the snow looked at that moment."

Stroud normally speaks softly, but his voice pinches to a whisper when he mentions Don's family. "My stomach still hurts when I think how many times I told them that I'd meet up with them to talk about the avalanche. My intentions were good. But I had survived, and Don and Bill had not. Really, I was scared to go back there. I don't know if I had the energy to be supportive."

Stroud feels as though he lost the two months immediately following his burial. "I just missed life for a while. I couldn't remember having specific conversations; I kept losing track of time. It was almost as though I was in a drug state. I'm not even sure why. It wasn't the first time I'd almost died; I bet most people don't think about how close to death they are every time they drive down the highway."

Ironically, the experience of being trapped ultimately offered Stroud greater freedom. "I look more critically at what I'm doing," he says, "and do more of what I think I need." Even more than a year later, the avalanche still runs through his mind several times a day. "A lot of different things went wrong, like the dogs dropped into the gully ahead of me and I didn't keep my distance from Skip. But enough little factors went right . . . ," he says, turning aside to wipe tears from the pond of his felt-brown eyes.

■   ■   ■

"It sucks being in a wheelchair," Nick Coltman said without a trace of self-pity when we spoke in his office nearly three years after his accident. "Everything is much more of an ordeal now, even just getting onto the couch or into a car. I get more attention than I deserve. I'm often ushered to the head of a line, even though I can wait as well as the next person—after all, I've got a chair."

From his window, he can see Flattop Mountain, and the accident still fast-forwards through his head all the time. "I'm not bitter or angry; it's just something that happened. I could have slipped in the bathtub or gotten into a car accident. What I miss the most is the crucible of friendship that comes from going out into the mountains with a bunch of friends. My friends miss it too; I think a lot of them are more depressed about what happened than I am." As he spoke, I was reminded of a passage in Wallace Stegner's novel *Crossing to Safety:* "Long-continued disability makes some people saintly, some self-pitying, some bitter. It has only clarified Sally and made her more herself." Nick Coltman radiates that same buoying clarity.

While we talked, an aging Boozer lay dreaming on the floor, and Maggie, also a mainstay at the *Anchorage Press,* could be seen through a plate-glass window. "I've always been fast and lucky," said Coltman, "and able to get myself out of jams. But that day my luck ran out." He paused, creating a silence that was not awkward or even sad. "Actually, I'm lucky as hell. I should be dead. I don't think I could have come back if I'd been any closer to that line."

OUT OF THE SHADOWS

JOHN HAINES

You'll have to hike a lot of wilderness trails and make your way through many shelves of books to meet up with a man like John Haines. He is not only an acclaimed poet and writer, published in magazines and books, but has spent a great deal of his life living in the Alaska wilds, on his own while trapping, hunting, fishing—surviving. This chapter from Haines's classic book The Stars, The Snow, The Fire, *subtitled "Twenty-Five Years in the Northern Wilderness," walks us through a dangerous encounter Haines was lucky to live to tell about. All Haines's books deserve a spot on your library shelves beside such outdoor literature greats as Jack London, Barry Lopez, Henry Beston, Annie Dillard, Sigurd Olson, and Farley Mowat. You don't have to take my word for it. Follow John Haines into the shadows, and you'll see what I mean.*

■   ■   ■

It was early in July. I was on my way to Cabin Creek, eight miles distant by trail in the Redmond drainage. I intended to make a quick overnight trip to secure our hunting cabin for the season and to see what the prospects might be for blueberries later that summer.

For company I had brought with me our youngest dog, a female husky named Moppet. She was nearly two years old, a quiet, alert and intelligent animal. Glad to be along, to have been chosen, she trotted ahead of me on the trail, the thick grey and white plume of her tail swinging from side to side.

I was carrying my big pack basket containing a small axe, some food, and an old sweater to wear in the evening. I was also carrying one of the two rifles I owned, an ancient 8mm Mannlicher carbine I had inherited from an old resident in the country. It had once been a fighting weapon of the German Army in World War I. It had a scarred stock and a worn barrel, but was compact and light and easy to carry.

We had left home early to take advantage of the morning coolness. Now, five miles out, with the sun high at our backs on the open, sloping bench above Redmond Creek, the mid-morning was clear and warm. As always here, the trail was wet underfoot, the moss and the dark sod still soaking from the spring runoff. Mosquitoes and small gnats rose out of the moss; a continual and shifting cloud of them swarmed about us.

As we walked along, skirting one dark pool of melt-water after another, I was thinking of many things: of the summer before me, of the fishing about to begin, the hoped-for success of the summer garden, and not too far ahead another hunting season. I took casual note of the places where in the winter just past I had set my traps: a shelter of twigs and sticks fallen together, and every so often under the lower boughs of a spruce tree standing near the trail a rusty marten trap was hanging, wired to its toggle stick.

It was a typical summer day in the subarctic backcountry. I was alone with a dog in a country that with its creeks, ridges and divides, and with the high, brown slope of Banner Dome visible to the north, was as familiar to me as any suburban backyard. On the changing features of the landscape I seemed to see written my own signature of use.

We rounded the steep spruce-clad prow of the hill above Glacier Creek and stopped briefly at a cache I kept there below the point of hill. Here, three years before and late in the fall, we had camped in a tent while hunting moose. The ground poles of our tent were lying where we had left them under the trees. It was not hard for me to visualize things as they had been then: the grey slope of the canvas tent, smoke from the stovepipe and snow in the wind. For a few weeks that tent had been home. Moppet was not yet born. Now I looked up at the narrow platform of the cache fixed solidly in the three spruces above me. A half dozen traps were hanging from a spike in one of the supports. The ridge pole of the tent and the rest of its framework were pitched together and standing upright against the cache to keep them dry. I saw that everything was as I had left it when I stopped here with the dogs and sled on the last snow of the season.

We left the cache and went on down the trail toward the creek. The brush was thick, of dense, small-statured black spruce interspersed with thickets of alders. The trail wound about so that at no time could I see more than thirty feet ahead of me. Moppet was now out of sight somewhere ahead and probably waiting for me at the crossing.

As I came out of the woods and onto the open bench above the creek, I saw Moppet sitting at the edge of the steep slide down which the trail led to the creek bottom. Her ears were pricked sharply forward, and she was staring intently at something in the creek.

When I came up to her, I saw what she was watching. Down in the creek and less than twenty yards away, the shoulders and back of a large brown animal showed above the heavy summer grass and clumps of ice-cropped willows. It was moving slowly downstream at the far edge of an island that divided the creek.

At first I thought the animal was a young moose feeding on the fresh grass or on some waterplants in the shallow streamcourse. And yet there was something about its size and bulk and the way that it was moving that was not quite familiar. And then the creature's head came into partial view, and I saw how the brown hump of its shoulders rippled as it moved. It was a bear, larger than any bear I had yet seen in that country. One look at that heavy square head and the shoulder hump, and I knew we had met a grizzly.

No more than a minute passed as I stood there with Moppet at my feet, watching the big bear in the grass below us. I was glad now that I had not brought one of our other dogs who would have immediately rushed barking into the creek after the bear. I was grateful for this quiet and obedient animal sitting at my feet with her hair stiffened on her shoulders and her nose twitching.

Where I stood at that moment I had an easy shot broadside into the bear's chest or shoulders. I could perhaps have killed it then and there. But I did not want to leave a dead bear to rot in the creek, and we were too far from home to pack out more than a small portion of the meat.

In the brief time that we stood there, I quickly went over my choices. We could not proceed down into the creek and follow the trail across to the opposite bank; the bear was by now directly in our path. We could stay where we were and let the bear go on downstream if that was its intention. But would Moppet remain quiet long enough?

I thought of easing away from the scene, of moving upstream far enough to cross without disturbing the bear. It would have to be done quickly and quietly. At any moment the bear might discover us, or the noise of our retreat might alarm it. In an emergency there were no trees large enough to climb, and there was no hope of outrunning an aroused bear in that wet and spongy ground. My one advantage lay in the fact that we were above the bear and that it had not yet discovered us.

But the bear soon left me no choice. Something in our unseen presence on the bank above the creek, some sound, some prickling sense that it was not alone, seemed to change the bear's intentions. It stopped feeding. Its head came up, and it began to move more rapidly through the grass. As it did so, it turned in our direction. It was now in full view, no more than fifty feet away, and closing the distance between us.

In my sudden alarm that grizzly loomed larger and more of a threat than any black bear or bull moose I had ever met with. I was ready to fire, but in those swift moments I thought I might be able to frighten the bear, and by some noise or movement scare it back into the woods. Still holding my rifle, I raised my arms over my head. In what seems now to have been a ridiculous gesture, I waved my arms and did a small dance on the moss; I yelled and hooted and hoped. But the sudden noise, coming out of the stillness, seemed only to panic the animal. It broke into a loping run, heading directly toward us, and had already reached the bottom of the bank below us. I had no choice now. I put the rifle to my shoulder, took hurried aim at the heavy chest of hair below that big head, and fired.

At the sound of the gunshot the bear abruptly stopped a few feet below. It rose on its hind legs and stood at full height in front of us. In a rush of images I saw the stocky, upright length of its body, a patch of pale fur on its underthroat, the forepaws raised in a defensive gesture; I saw the blunt muzzle and the suddenly opened jaws. The bear growled loudly, swung its head to one side, and tried to bite at its chest. I was ready to fire again, and at that moment I might have put a shot squarely into its thick neck or broad upper chest. But for some reason in those tense seconds I again held my fire.

The bear dropped back to the ground. It turned away from us and ran back through the grass and brush in a tremendous, lunging gallop, scattering leaves and splashing water. I watched it climb the bank on the opposite side of the creek and disappear. A heavy crashing came from the dry alders on the far side, and then all was still.

I stood at the top of the bank with my rifle half-raised, listening. Over everything in that sudden stillness I was aware of my heart as a loud pounding above the calm trickle of water in the creek below. I heard a low whine, and glanced down. All this time Moppet had remained crouched and quiet at my feet. But now she rose with her hair bristling, searching the air with her nose, trying to catch some scent of that enormous creature so suddenly discovered and now vanished.

I moved away from the trail and walked a short distance upstream to where a bulky, crooked spruce grew at the edge of the bank. It was as large as any tree in the vicinity, and for some reason I felt more comfortable standing close to it. I removed my pack and set it on the ground beside me. I placed my rifle against the tree while I searched in my shirt pocket for tobacco and papers. In those days I was an occasional smoker. With trembling hands I rolled a cigarette, lit it, and smoked in silence.

It had all happened so quickly. Perhaps no more than three minutes had elapsed since I had first seen the bear. Now that I had some space in which to think, I realized that

I had been extremely lucky. Had the bear not stopped, a second shot might have killed it, but if not there would have been no way I could have escaped at least a severe mauling.

Somehow in that blur of excitement and indecision, I knew that I would not turn and run. Out of whatever stubborn sense of my own right to be there, or simply from an obscure pride, I would stand my ground, fire my shot, and from then on fend off the wounded bear as best I could, using my rifle for a club. In that event I would most likely have been killed, or I would have been so badly maimed that I could never have made it home without help, and there was no help anywhere near. Days might have passed before anyone came looking for me.

I stood there and smoked, gradually coming to some calm in myself. I could hear nothing from the woods on the far side of the creek. There was not the slightest movement to be seen in the brush growing upon that low bank, nothing at all in the grass below. From time to time I gazed up or down the creek as far as I could see above the willows and alders. Nothing.

I did not know how badly hit that bear was. Perhaps it was now lying dead over there. Or it might only be wounded, lying in the brush near the trail, gathering its strength and waiting for me to pass. At such times events and probabilities seemed magnified; fear has a thousand faces.

I finished my cigarette, and picked up my pack and my rifle. I knew that I would have to go down into the creek and search the sand and grass for blood. Whatever I found, I would follow the bear's path across the creek and into the woods. I wanted above all to be on my way to the cabin and out of any further trouble. But first I had to be sure of that bear.

I waited another few minutes. Then, with Moppet at my heels, I returned to the trail, and we began our descent into the creek.

At the bottom of the bank I easily found the place where the bear had stood up after I fired at him. His big tracks were pressed deeply into the wet sand, the long toenails and the pad marks clearly outlined at the edge of the small channel.

Slowly and quietly I began to trace the bear's path through the grass. Stopping frequently to look around me over the grass and through the brush, I followed as well as I could the paw marks in the sand and the muddy sod. Where I could not see his tracks, I guided myself by the bent and broken grasses in the deep trough of the bear's passage. As I walked, half-crouched, searching the ground, I examined with care every blade of grass and every leaf on the willows. But I found no sign of blood.

We went on through the grass and brush. Across the far channel we found the trail, climbed the shallow bank and entered the woods. Moppet remained at my heels, at times pressing closely against my leg. Though I tried quietly to coax her, she would not go ahead but stayed close behind. The hair on her shoulders and neck was stiffened, and as she looked from side to side into the woods a muted and anxious throaty sound came from her, half growl and half whine.

Once up the bank and into the woods, we stopped. It was spooky as hell under that shadowy, sun-broken canopy of leaves. I searched the woods around me for the slightest movement and listened for any sound: wounded breathing, a growl, anything. Nowhere in all that wilderness could I hear a sound above the muted purling of water in the creek behind me, and the song of a fox sparrow somewhere in the watercourse.

We walked on, following the trail where it skirted the edge of a narrow ravine holding a wayward tributary of the creek. To cross the ravine I had built a rough bridge out of spruce poles. On the far side the trail turned upstream and continued through a swamp toward Cabin Creek.

When Moppet and I had crossed the bridge, I stopped again. Here an old game trail, deeply-cut into the moss, intersected our sled trail and took its narrow, twisting way downstream. I hesitated. Nothing I had seen so far convinced me that the bear was at all wounded, but I was still not satisfied. I stepped into the game trail and began a careful circuit of the downstream woods into which I had seen the bear vanish. As quiet as it was, as eerily still, I felt that somewhere in that dim tangle of alders, willows and dwarf birch the bear must be lying and listening to our movements. As in an episode of warfare, a pervasive uneasiness seemed to divide the shadows and the sunlight. I had that acute sense of being watched and listened to by an invisible foe. Each twig-snap and wave of a bough seemed a potential signal.

After about twenty minutes of what I considered to be a reasonably careful search, I returned to the trail. I now felt, from the lack of any bloodsign or other evidence, that the bear had not been badly hit. I decided not to pursue the search any further. With Moppet following me, I went on through the swamp, climbing steadily toward the saddle that divided Glacier from Cabin Creek. We went carefully, every so often stopping to look back down the trail behind us. We were well away from the creek before Moppet would put aside her fear and go ahead of me.

It seemed to me now that I had merely grazed the underside of the bear's chest. I had fired downhill at a running target, and had aimed low. Moreover, the front sight of the old carbine had been damaged years ago and repaired with solder in a makeshift fashion. The gunsight was uncertain at best.

So obviously I had fired too low, and the bear had suffered no more than a nasty sting from the heavy 230 grain bullet I was using. Had the bear been solidly hit, there would surely have been blood somewhere, and there would by now be a dead or dying bear in the woods. As we came down off the hill on the last half mile stretch to the cabin I began to feel a great deal easier, satisfied that I had not left a badly wounded animal behind me, and glad too that we had gotten off from the encounter ourselves with no more trouble.

■ ■ ■

We spent the night at the cabin. I fed Moppet and cut some firewood. In the late afternoon I did a few needed chores about the cabin. On going to the creek for a bucket of water, I found a few unripe blueberries among the bushes overhanging the deep, wet moss hummocks beside the creek. The berries were scattered, and it did not seem to me that they would be worth a trip later to pick them. As the evening light deepened over the hills and the air grew cooler, a thrush sent up its spiraling song from the aspens on the hillside across the creek. Mosquitoes whined at the screen door. Otherwise, things were very quiet there on the hill above Cabin Creek.

The following morning I secured the cabin for the remainder of the summer. I set a strong barricade over the door, and closed and nailed heavy shutters over the two windows. In the late morning Moppet and I set out for home.

As we came down through the swamp near Glacier, Moppet once more dropped behind me and refused to go ahead. I walked quietly with the rifle safety off and my hand half-closed on the trigger. Again I watched the brush and listened to either side of the trail for the slightest sound. There was nothing but the quiet sunlit air of a summer day.

We crossed the creek, striding the small channels and pushing aside the grass, and on the far side we climbed the bank again. When we came to the top, I looked down. There, squarely in the trail and almost exactly where I had stood the day before when I fired at the bear, was a fresh mound of bear droppings. Nearby lay the spent shell from my rifle.

I looked closely at the dropping. It contained a few unripe blueberries, seeds and other matter. It was still wet, though not warm. Moppet sniffed at it, and the grizzled hair once more rose on her neck and shoulders. For a moment my uneasiness returned, that vague, shivery sense of being watched and followed. The bear was still around, alive and well. Dangerous? I had no way of knowing.

The bear had probably not run far on the previous day, but had found a place in which to lie and lick its wound, baffled as to the source of its sudden hurt. It had heard us pass on the trail, had heard every sound of my passage in the brush, had followed every detail of my search. Perhaps much later in the evening it came out of its hiding place, out of the late cool shadows, and returned to the trail. It had stood where we were standing now, with its great, shaggy head down, sniffing the moss, the wet, black sod, trying to place in its dim sense of things an identity it would carry with it for the rest of its life.

I looked back down into the grass and brush of the creek from which we had just come. I turned and looked ahead of me to where the stubby black spruce wood closed in around the trail. If the bear was still somewhere in that dense green cover, nursing its hurt and its temper, waiting for revenge, it would have its chance.

But nothing vengeful and bloody came out of the woods to meet us as we went on up the trail. The walk home by Redmond, the long uphill climb to the homestead ridge passed without further incident. We came down off the hill as on many another occasion, to the sunlit vista of the river and the highway, to the sound of the dogs' furious barking. I had a good story to tell, and Moppet was petted and praised for her wise behavior.

In many subsequent hikes over the trail to Cabin Creek, in hunting forays along the benches above Glacier, we never saw that bear again. Now and then in late summer and early fall a blue mound of dropping in the trail gave evidence of a bear in the country, and that was all.

Never before or since have I been so rattled on meeting an animal in the woods. Years later, when I began to think of writing these pages, I rehearsed for myself another outcome to the adventure. I described in detail how the bear, badly hit in its lungs, had waited in the brush on the far side of the creek. When Moppet and I went by on the trail, the bear suddenly lunged from its hiding place with a terrible, bubbling roar and struck me down.

In that instant of confusion and shock I was joined to the hot blood and rank fur at last. All my boyhood dreams of life in the woods, of courage and adventure, had come to this final and terrifying intimacy.

Following the initial shock, as I lay sprawled by the trail with the bear standing hot and wounded above me, I managed to regain a grip on my rifle. Though stunned and, as it seemed, half blinded, I raised the short muzzle of than ancient weapon and got off one last shot into the bear's throat. And with the sound of that shot in my ears, I lost consciousness.

In what may have been an hour or only minutes, I returned to a dazed sense of myself. I sat up, struggling to free myself of the things that seemed to hold me: my pack harness, torn clothing, and bits of broken brush. I seemed to look at myself and my surroundings from a great distance through a sun-dazzled semi-darkness. I was still alive, though in the numbed, head-ringing silence I knew I was hurt, badly cut and bitten about my face and body. Moppet was gone. A short distance away from me the bear lay dead.

Somehow, maimed, stiffened and bleeding, using a dry stick for a crutch, I found my way home. Patched and scarred, I wore my changed face as an emblem of combat, and walked in my damaged body to the end of my days, survivor of a meeting terrible and true.

COPYRIGHTS AND PERMISSIONS

ABOUT THE EDITOR

Lamar Underwood is a former editor-in-chief of *Sports Afield* and *Outdoor Life* and has been a prolific editor of anthologies and other books for Lyons Press and Globe Pequot Press.

Lamar's novel *On Dangerous Ground* draws considerably on his experiences as a magazine editor in New York and his outdoor experiences in Alaska when his father was stationed there during the Korean War.

Several of Lamar's previous anthologies have focused on adventure and survival in the great outdoors. These include *The Greatest Adventure Stories Ever Told* and *The Greatest Survival Stories Ever Told*, both published by Lyons and Globe Pequot Press. He also was the editor of *Classic Survival Stories*, *Basic Wilderness Survival Skills*, *Man Eaters*, and *The Greatest Disaster Stories Ever Told*.

Lamar's other anthologies for Lyons Press cover a wide range of subjects, including war, hunting, fishing, submarines, flying, mountain men, and Theodore Roosevelt's hunting tales. He also wrote two books of quotations for Lyons Press: *The Quotable Soldier* and *The Quotable Writer*.

Lamar's articles on the outdoors appear in magazines such as *Field & Stream*. Other recent books include *1001 Fishing Secrets* and (coauthor with Nate Matthews) *1001 Hunting Secrets*.